MW01506143

Stray Wives

Stray Wives

Marital Conflict in
Early National New England

Mary Beth Sievens

NEW YORK UNIVERSITY PRESS
New York and London

NEW YORK UNIVERSITY PRESS
New York and London
www.nyupress.org

Library of Congress Cataloging-in-Publication Data
Sievens, Mary Beth.
Stray wives : marital conflict in early national New England / Mary
Beth Sievens.
p. cm.
Includes bibliographical references and index.
ISBN-13: 978-0-8147-4009-5 (cloth : alk. paper)
ISBN-10: 0-8147-4009-X (cloth : alk. paper)
1. Marital conflict—New England—History—18th century. 2.
Marital conflict—New England—History—19th century. 3.
Wives—New England—History. 4. Husband and wife—New Eng-
land—History. 5. Legal advertising—New England—History. I.
Title.
HQ537.S54   2005
306.872'0974'09034—dc22   2005010577

New York University Press books are printed on acid-free paper,
and their binding materials are chosen for strength and durability.

Portions of chapters 1 and 3 first appeared in Mary Beth Sievens,
"Divorce, Patriarchal Authority, and Masculinity: A Case from Early
National Vermont," *Journal of Social History* 37 (Spring 2004):
651–61. Additional portions of chapter 3 first appeared in Mary
Beth Sievens, "'The Fruit of My Industry': Economic Roles and Mar-
ital Conflict in New England, 1790–1830," in *Women's Work in
New England, 1620–1920*, Annual Proceedings of the Dublin Semi-
nar for New England Folklife, 2001, ed. Peter Benes (Boston: Boston
University Press, 2003), 68–77. Portions of chapter 4 first appeared
in Mary Beth Sievens, "'The Wicked Agency of Others': Community,
Law, and Marital Conflict in Vermont, 1790–1830," *Journal of the
Early Republic* 21 (Spring 2001): 19–39; reprinted by permission of
the University of Pennsylvania Press.

Manufactured in the United States of America
10 9 8 7 6 5 4 3 2 1

For Christopher and Joshua Goodhue

Contents

List of Tables

Acknowledgments

I am delighted to finally have the opportunity to thank the individuals and institutions that provided invaluable assistance as I worked on this project. The Boston University Humanities Foundation provided crucial financial support when I began my research, as did two Mount Holyoke College Class of 1905 Research Fellowships. A Kate B. and Hall J. Peterson Fellowship made possible an extremely fruitful research trip to the American Antiquarian Society. SUNY Fredonia provided travel funds to support my research and release time to create a database for statistical analysis. I owe thanks to many people at the libraries and archives I visited as I conducted research. The librarians and support staffs at the Connecticut Historical Society, Connecticut State Library, New England Historic Genealogical Society, Vermont Historical Society, Vermont State Library, General Services Center of the State of Vermont, and the Special Collections Archives of the Bailey-Howe Library at the University of Vermont helped locate materials and provided cheerful assistance when microfilm "exploded" off reels and when I (inevitably) jammed photocopy machines. Special thanks to Caroline Sloat, Joanne Chaison, Marie Lamoureux, Dennis Laurie, the late Joyce Tracy, and other staff members at the American Antiquarian Society for providing a congenial, supportive atmosphere in which to research and for always welcoming me back when I returned to search through their collections yet again.

The scholars who commented on this manuscript have improved it in numerous ways. Norma Basch, Nancy Cott, Hendrik Hartog, Randy Roth, and Lisa Wilson read and commented on portions of this work as conference papers, articles, or chapters. The readers at New York University Press made invaluable suggestions that helped me strengthen the manuscript. Kirsten Sword generously shared with me her findings on marital conflict and the legal standing of elopement notices in the colonial era. Nina Dayton provided very helpful tips on research in early Connecticut records. Richard and Irene Brown's interest in and support of this project have been a constant source of encouragement. Nina Silber, Marilyn Halter, Bruce Schulman, and Laurel Ulrich read the manuscript when it was still a dissertation. Their questions and comments helped guide me as I conducted further research and revised the manuscript. I owe a special debt of gratitude to Alan Taylor, who provided the perfect mix of encouragement, criticism, and townball throughout graduate school and as I labored on the dissertation. The example of his high standards and rigorous scholarship constantly push me to improve my own work. I have been very fortunate to work with Deborah Gershenowitz at New York University Press. Her enthusiasm for this project, as well as the efficiency of NYUP's editorial staff, has made the publication process as stress-free as possible.

I also am grateful to several friends and family members for their help as I worked on this project. My parents, Robert and Patricia Sievens, endured many "home invasions" whenever I needed to visit the New England Historic Genealogical Society or the American Antiquarian Society. Steve and Debbie Reige always made me feel at home when my research travels took me to Hartford, Connecticut. My sister, Kathleen Oliver, provided research assistance and companionship as I worked in Connecticut sources. My colleagues in the History Department at SUNY Fredonia have encouraged me and offered helpful advice as I transformed the dissertation into a book. Finally, researching and writing about marital conflict for more than ten years would have been unbearable had it not been for my own tranquil and happy family life. For that I thank my husband, Christopher Goodhue, and our son, Joshua. I dedicate this book to them.

Introduction

On January 13, 1796, a husband and wife each placed an advertisement in the Bennington *Vermont Gazette*. In one advertisement, Enoch Darling announced, "Whereas Phebe Darling my wife, hath eloped from my bed and board, and refuses to return to duty I therefore forbid all persons harboring or trusting her on my account, as I will not pay any debts of her contracting after this date." In the other notice, Phebe Darling explained her own version of the couple's marital difficulties:

> Whereas my husband, Enoch Darling, has at sundry times used me in so improper and cruel a manner, as to destroy my happiness and endanger my life, and whereas he has not provided for me as a husband ought, but expended his time and money unadvisedly, at taverns, to the detriment of myself and his family. I hereby notify the public that I am obliged to leave him, and shall henceforth pay no debts of his contracting on any account whatever, as heretofore I have done.

Hundreds of these elopement notices appeared in New England newspapers between 1790 and 1830, testifying to the marital difficulties that many couples experienced and raising questions about the nature of the marriage relationship in early national New England. Ordinary men and women detailed their marital expectations and experiences in elopement notices. Their advertisements demonstrate that tensions existed within the legal framework that governed marriage and between that framework and the actual relationships that husbands and wives constructed. The law granted husbands considerable authority over their dependent, subordinate wives. However, the content of desertion notices reveals that, in reality, neither husbands' authority nor wives' subordination was as absolute as a strict reading of the doctrine of marital unity would indicate.

1

Instead, married couples had to negotiate the meaning of husbands' superior status and wives' dependence.[1]

Elopement notices provide a window into that negotiation process. These advertisements present an opportunity to study men's and women's understandings of the marriage contract as defined by the common law, as well as their perceptions of the day-to-day realities of marriage. Elopement notices reveal the opportunities available to men and women of the early republic to shape their marriages. The notices demonstrate the legal advantages that husbands held over their wives. Men used the notices to control their wives' consumer behavior and to pressure their spouses to submit to their authority. However, the notices also reveal that wives had considerable bargaining power within the marriage relationship. Because of the importance of wives' labors to the household economy, their desertions could make it difficult for their husbands to prosper. On March 1, 1806, Levi Priest reported the desertion of his wife, Sally, and complained that she had "left me with four small children to maintain." He then attempted to convince Sally to return: "If said Sally will return and help me to maintain our children, I hereby engage to give her 30 Dollars —and good usage as her heart can wish." Husbands such as Levi Priest had the legal power to deny their wives credit; however, when they left their husbands, wives such as Sally Priest displayed a certain power of their own. When Sally eloped, Levi realized how important her labors were and he was willing to pay her to return. Wives like Sally Priest were aware of the importance of their household labors, and deserting was one way they could demonstrate that importance to their husbands. As the Priests' example reveals, elopement notices offer a way to explore how men and women perceived and tried to negotiate the balance of power within their marriages.[2]

Husbands such as Enoch Darling and Levi Priest posted these notices to deprive their wives of access to their credit with merchants, artisans, and other community members. According to William Blackstone's commentaries on the common law, a married woman was a *feme covert,* one whose legal existence was "suspended during the marriage, or at least, is incorporated and consolidated into that of the husband." Upon marrying, a woman could not own property, claim her own wages, or enter into contracts in her own name. Married women were not legally liable for their own debts: according to the common law, these were the responsibility of their husbands. However, if a woman eloped from her husband, the law allowed him to refuse to pay her debts. Darling and Priest used this power when they printed their elopement notices. Husbands' newspaper postings were patriarchal tools that emphasized married women's economic dependence. Credit was essential in the cash-scarce New England economy in the early national period; depriving a woman of the ability to charge items to her husband's accounts could leave her without any means of support. Husbands could use their legal power to grant and withdraw credit to punish their errant wives and to coerce them into returning and behaving as the men wished. Without access to her husband's credit and without any other means of support, a "posted" wife might have no other option than to return to her husband and submit to his will. In this context, Priest's offer of thirty dollars to his wife if she returned was a "carrot" that complemented the "stick," her loss of access to her husband's credit if she remained apart from him.[3]

When men wrote that their wives had eloped, they used "elope" in a context that differed from today's meaning of the word. Darling, Priest, and their contemporaries would have recognized the modern use of "elope" to mean lovers running away to get married. However, they held a broader definition of the word, one that encompassed the actions of runaway servants, children, and wives. In the colonial era and in the early national period, to elope meant to run away. When men advertised their wives' elopements, the term had illicit connotations. Because women were legally dependent on men, a notice implied that any woman who had left her husband's bed and board must be receiving support from another man. Indeed, legal commentators such as William Blackstone and James Kent often assumed that women lived with other men after eloping. Men's advertisements sometimes appeared in newspapers under the heading "Stray Wives," a term that referred to the women's desertions as well as to any sexual transgressions they may have committed. Not all eloped wives had strayed sexually; however, women who left their husbands' homes were vulnerable to the charge of sexual misconduct that elopement notices implied.[4]

Enoch Darling's notice reveals that husbands held a tremendous amount of legal power over their wives. However, Phebe's notice demonstrates that, in spite of their subordinate legal status, married women had access to resources and opportunities to act in their own interests. The Darlings' notices illuminate some of the contradictions inherent in the common law of marriage. Enoch Darling's notice reveals his legal ability to deny his wife credit; yet, in her notice, Phebe demonstrated a keen awareness of wives' legal rights. If a husband's cruel behavior forced a wife to leave his home, legally she remained entitled to his support. Did Enoch have the right to deny Phebe access to his credit, or did his cruel behavior justify her desertion and entitle her to his support? Both Enoch and Phebe appealed to the common law in support of their marital rights, and in the process their notices help reveal some of the ambiguities of that law. Their notices also reveal the contradictions that could exist between law and lived experience. The law recognized Enoch Darling as a household head who controlled his family's economic assets and assumed responsibility for his family's economic support. However, the products of women's labors—such as cloth and cheese—often paid families' debts at local stores, enabling Phebe Darling to claim that, in reality, she had paid Enoch's debts. Enoch Darling believed that he had the law on his side when he wrote his elopement notice, but Phebe Darling had so strong a sense of her legal rights as a wife that she challenged her husband publicly and defied his authority over her in spite of her dependent status.[5]

Despite the rich content and the ubiquity of elopement notices, historians have paid them scant attention.[6] Many scholars have explored the legal structures that shaped the marriage relationship. They have analyzed legal commentators' pronouncements on the implications of *feme covert* status for married women's ability to own and devise property, to conduct their own businesses, and to earn their own wages. Studies of divorce law, child custody law, and proceedings in courts of equity have provided clues to women's status and opportunities.[7] In addition, numerous historians have analyzed cultural ideals regarding marriage, the family, and women's proper role in society, while others have produced an impressive body of scholarship examining economic relations within the family and the ways in which economic changes affected women's activities and status.[8]

The work done by these scholars points to the late eighteenth and early nineteenth centuries as an important transitional period in terms of cultural ideals, as well as women's legal and economic position within the family. In the early republic, a new companionate ideal highlighting affection, mutuality, and greater equality between husbands and wives was replacing more traditional, hierarchical marriage norms. Greater intimacy and companionship between spouses promised to soften the harsher edges of traditional patriarchal authority. At the same time, notions of a separate "woman's sphere" elevated female influence and prestige within the home by highlighting women's uniquely nurturing, moral, and religious nature. These cultural shifts were linked to dramatic economic changes occurring in the early decades of the republic. Increasing involvement in an expanding market economy eventually would transform the household economy in radical ways. Production shifted away from the household to the work place, reorienting women's domestic economic roles toward consumer activities and buttressing the notion that married women's most important task was caring for and training their children.

The scholars who analyze these cultural and economic transformations differ in their assessments of how these changes affected women's status. Some argue that notions of a separate woman's sphere provided women with an important source of dignity and power within the home, as well as a sense of sisterhood that would serve as a foundation for future women's rights organizations. Other historians emphasize the restrictive nature of women's domestic sphere and the devaluation of women's household labors that resulted from the heightened importance attached to men's wage-earning activities and women's role as mothers. The varied assessments of women's status that these historians offer serve to highlight the uneven, transitional nature of the cultural and economic changes occurring in the late eighteenth and early nineteenth centuries.[9] In spite of this lack of consensus regarding the effects of these transformations in family ideals and the household economy, it is clear that these changes existed in tension with a legal code of marriage that continued to support a tremendous imbalance of power between husbands and wives. Some legal change did occur in the late eighteenth and early nineteenth centuries: more liberal divorce laws made it easier for women and men to exit broken marriages, and some scholars have identified legal trends that allowed married women greater control over property. However, the common law of coverture remained essentially unchanged until the mid-nineteenth century, when state statutes and court decisions regarding married women's property and wages, child custody, wives' contractual and testamentary abilities, and inheritance would significantly modify (but not eliminate) husbands' superior legal position within marriage and the family.[10]

In this study, I ask how ordinary men and women perceived, used, and lived with the common law of marriage in an era of exceptional cultural and economic change. I take as my starting point Hendrik Hartog's complex assessment of coverture and its effects on married women. Hartog argues that although coverture maintained a power structure that favored husbands, it did not erase wives' legal identities and rights. Rather, coverture created a particular identity for married women, vested with legally specific duties and privileges. Wives owed their husbands obedience and their labor; however, wives also had the right to adequate economic support and kind treatment. Coverture mandated certain rights, as well as certain limitations, for both married men and married women.[11]

The transitional nature of the decades at the end of the eighteenth and beginning of the nineteenth centuries provides an ideal opportunity to assess the ways in which couples negotiated the common law of marriage, as well as cultural and economic changes regarding the roles of husbands and wives and the meaning of marriage. Newspaper postings provide an excellent window into these issues because they help reveal husbands' and wives' perceptions of the law, of marital ideals, of lived experience, and of the relationships among these factors. Elopement notices contain many formulaic elements—from statements claiming that the author did nothing to provoke his or her marital discord to the inclusion of standard complaints against the offending spouse. These advertisements are not objective descriptions of troubled early national marriages. Instead, notice authors shaped their particular experiences into a narrative that would be legally compelling and persuasive to other community members. The resulting formulaic elements of the postings are important because they help to identify the acceptance of certain conventions regarding marriage ideals and the proper behavior of husbands and wives. However, couples could use these conventions to mask less socially acceptable sources of marital dissatisfaction. Given the strengths and limitations of elopement notices as sources, I use evidence ranging from legal treatises, law suits, and divorce cases to sermons and prescriptive literature to place the evidence about marital conflict that the postings provide into a broader context of cultural ideals, as well as legal doctrine and practice.

Men and women crafted their notices to appeal to legal norms; yet, the actual legal status of the postings appears to have been uncertain. The authors of legal treatises agreed that when wives eloped without cause, their husbands had the right to alert merchants that they would no longer pay the women's debts. However, these authors did not address the question of whether a newspaper advertisement was sufficient notification to legally oblige merchants to deny estranged wives credit. The various legal handbooks that appeared in the eighteenth and nineteenth centuries to advise ordinary people on proper legal forms and procedures offered conflicting assessments of the notices. Some maintained that newspaper postings were not sufficient legal notification, while others included examples of elopement notices as proper legal forms.[12]

This legal uncertainty may not have been especially troubling to couples; in fact, the ambiguous legal standing of the notices may have served husbands' and wives' varied and contradictory purposes well. When husbands published desertion notices, they hoped to avoid responsibility for their wives' debts; however, many also hoped their notices would persuade their wives to reconcile. Likewise, wives who printed notices hoped that their countercharges would convince merchants to allow them continued access to their husbands' credit. Many also wished their notices would encourage neighbors and other community members to pressure their spouses to change their ways and make possible a reunion. In contrast, some men and women intended their postings to notify their communities that they had separated permanently and would no longer fulfill their marital obligations to one another. Newspaper notices could serve all of these purposes, in part because of their uncertain legal standing. Had legislators and jurists defined the notices' form and function, they would have narrowed the ways that couples used the postings. Instead, the legal status of the notices remained vague, subject to the differing needs of estranged couples and to the expectations and interpretations of the communities in which these couples lived.

This work analyzes desertion postings found in Vermont and Connecticut newspapers between 1790 and 1830. It also examines the lives of a sample population of 175 men and women who wrote these notices. I focus on Windsor County, Vermont, and Hartford County, Connecticut, because, between them, these counties contained a mix of communities that typified the Northeast in the late eighteenth and early nineteenth centuries. At one end of this range of community types was Hartford, Connecticut, the largest urban area in either county. Established in 1635, with a population of over five thousand in 1810, Hartford's economy and population were the most diverse among the communities in this study. According to the 1820 census, 68 percent of the residents of the city of Hartford reported working in manufacturing. Twenty-five percent reported commerce as their occupation, while a mere 7 percent reported agriculture as their primary economic activity.[13] At the opposite end of the spectrum were towns like Ludlow, Vermont. A rural, farming community settled in 1783, Ludlow's population in 1800 was a mere 409 souls, a number that almost tripled by 1820 and then leveled off as residents struggled to make ends meet in the town's rather mountainous terrain.[14] In spite of this diversity of community size, type, and economy, the residents of Windsor and Hartford counties shared a growing involvement in New England's developing market economy. Greater involvement in the market increased the importance of such issues as debt, consumer spending, and productive labor, issues that were at the heart of many couples' marriage difficulties.

Connecticut and Vermont residents also shared several other characteristics and experiences. The residents of both counties were overwhelmingly Protestant and of Anglo descent, sharing a common cultural and religious heritage. In fact, a large proportion of Vermont's early settlers migrated from Connecticut, as the many shared place names in both counties indicate. The Connecticut migrants who settled in Vermont established a system of laws that was very similar to the Connecticut legal code. Many of the first laws enacted in Vermont were word-for-word copies of Connecticut statutes, and although differences in the two states' laws emerged over time, they did not erase the common legal culture that residents of Vermont and Connecticut shared. Vermont and Connecticut men and women used and interpreted elopement notices within a common legal context, one that was fairly lenient in its treatment of marital conflict. Vermont adopted Connecticut's divorce statute in 1779, allowing divorce on the grounds of adultery, fraudulent contract, three years' willful desertion, or seven years' absence without contact. This was a very lenient divorce law by late-eighteenth-century standards; by 1787, Vermont's law had become even more lenient, when legislators added intolerable severity to the list of grounds for which divorce could be sought. Yet, in spite of this relative leniency, other, less formal means of dealing with marital conflict persisted.[15]

The widespread use of elopement notices in two states with lenient divorce laws demonstrates that these notices were not mere substitutes for divorce. New England is an ideal place to analyze elopement notices precisely because couples had access to a broad range of methods for dealing with marital conflict, from informal separation to legal divorce. New England couples did not resort to using elopement notices because it was impossible for them to obtain divorces. In fact, the majority of accusations that spouses made against one another in their notices—desertion, adultery, and (in Vermont) cruelty—were legitimate grounds for divorce in these states. Between 1790 and 1830, Windsor County, Vermont, newspapers printed 317 elopement notices; the state supreme court heard 148 divorce petitions while sitting in the county between 1794 and 1825.

In Hartford County, Connecticut, newspapers published 461 notices between 1790 and 1830, while the state superior court heard 251 divorce petitions as it sat in the county during the same period. According to my research on a sample population of couples who printed notices, approximately one-third went on to divorce. Clearly, those couples who settled their marital disputes before the bar represent a minority of all estranged couples. The majority of spouses who published desertion notices chose not to divorce. They turned to elopement notices because they wanted to achieve different resolutions to their marriage conflicts. Perhaps they hoped to convince a spouse to change his or her ways so they could reconcile. Perhaps they hoped to remain legally married but to live separately. Elopement notices presented Connecticut and Vermont couples with a more flexible way to resolve their conflicts than did divorce.[16]

Although Vermont and Connecticut couples had access to lenient divorce laws and a variety of less formal practices when experiencing marital conflict, they did not have access to separate courts of chancery responsible for administering equity. Equity was a system of jurisprudence that ameliorated some of the disabilities married women faced under the common law. In particular, equity allowed married women to acquire separate estates, with varying degrees of control over property. Typically, the father of a married woman would convey property to a trustee, who was responsible for holding the property for the separate use and benefit of the woman and/or her heirs. Fathers did not intend these separate estates to provide their married daughters with greater independence; rather, their goal was to remove the control of property from incompetent or debt-ridden sons-in-law. However, when marital separation occurred, courts of chancery had the power to allow women to support themselves using their separate estates. New England colonies, and then states, did not establish separate Chancery Courts. As Marylynn Salmon explains in her study of women and early American property law, the Puritan founders of the New England colonies disliked the chancery court's elaborate, expensive procedures and lack of juries. Instead, the founders of these colonies empowered common law courts to act as courts of chancery in certain specific instances. However, because Puritans also disliked the challenge to the unity of interest between husband and wife that separate estates presented, they did not authorize common law courts to enforce such estates. As Salmon notes, separate estates were not necessarily illegal; however, if wives needed to turn to the courts to enforce such estates (a necessity that marital difficulties could provoke), they encountered an unsympathetic legal system. As a result of this procedural and ideological opposition, married women in New England confronted the common law without the mediating influence of equity jurisprudence in separate chancery courts.[17]

Vermont and Connecticut couples shared a common legal culture within which they used and interpreted elopement notices. They also shared an extremely high literacy rate. In his study of reading in early national Vermont, William Gilmore concludes that between 85 and 89 percent of men and between 70 and 82 percent of women were literate. Although no separate study of literacy exists for early national Connecticut, several studies persuasively argue that almost all colonial New Englanders could read, a rate that would not have declined by the early nineteenth century. In other words, the vast majority of Connecticut and Vermont men and women could read elopement notices, as well as write them, should the need arise. Because print culture was so widely accessible, it provides a very good lens through which to view ordinary people's perceptions of their marriages.[18]

This study begins with an analysis of the words New England men and women used to describe their marriages when they wrote desertion notices, and proceeds to an examination of the experiences of couples who published such announcements. Although both men and women were capable of writing desertion notices, men did so far more frequently than women. Vermont men posted 1,136 elopement notices between 1790 and 1830, while women published fifty-one advertisements detailing their versions of their marital conflicts. Hartford County, Connecticut, newspapers printed 446 notices written by husbands and fifteen notices written by wives. Women's advertisements account for only 4 percent of all postings. Most women who placed advertisements in newspapers did so in response to their husbands' notices. Fifty-four of the sixty-six New England women in this study posted notices to defend themselves against charges their husbands had published. Only twelve women appear to have placed advertisements without being provoked by their husbands' previous postings.[19] This vast disproportion between the number of men's and women's notices reflects husbands' privileged position within the marriage relationship. Aware of their superior status within marriage, husbands frequently used elopement notices to reassert their authority over wayward wives. Men readily exploited their legal power to deny their eloped wives access to their credit. In contrast, social conventions discouraged women from appearing in any public forum, making a wife's decision to publish a notice a difficult one. A woman who exposed her husband's inappropriate behavior in a newspaper might gain the support of neighbors, merchants, and local officials. However, such a public display also might reflect poorly on her own character. Because of this risk, women presented their stories infrequently, a hesitation that demonstrates the precarious status of estranged wives.

Married women were not powerless, however. One of the strengths of elopement notices is that they provide a rare opportunity to hear the voices of ordinary women recounting their expectations and experiences. The New England women and the men who wrote these notices represent a broad range of human experience, from wealthy merchants to indigent paupers reliant on poor relief, from urban artisans and laborers to farmers in rural outposts. Beginning in 1790, on the eve of Vermont statehood, and continuing to 1830, by which time the notices had become more formulaic and less revealing, this study explores the words and experiences of these New Englanders as they tried to shape the terms of their most significant social relationship.

1

A "Disobedient, Clamorous" Wife

The Problem of Wifely Submission

In 1802, the Reverend Martin Tullar, pastor of the Congregational Church in Royalton, Vermont, published a series of sermons entitled *A Concise System of Family Duty*. The first two sermons outlined the respective duties of husbands and wives. Tullar instructed husbands to provide a "comfortable subsistence" for their wives, to respect them, and to "treat them with great tenderness, and much forbearance." Turning to the proper role of wives, Tullar explained that "it is . . . incumbent on a wife, that she, with care, and diligence, improve those materials for family support, which may be committed to her instrument." The good wife was modest, neat, faithful, good-humored, and pious. She was "an help for the man, in all the cares, and concerns of life," and she continually worked to maintain "the comfort and prosperity . . . the good and well-being" of her family. These ideals and roles were not innovative. From the earliest days of colonial settlement, Puritan ministers had instructed husbands to support their wives economically and to treat them with kindness, while reminding wives to assist their husbands and to tend to their household duties diligently.[1]

Tullar also did not stray from accepted traditions when he described the ideal relationship between husbands and wives as one between a superior and a subordinate. However, like many ministers before him, Tullar qualified his description of the marital hierarchy: "in the divine arrangement of things, superiority was given to the man: yet, . . . it was not the design of his great Creator, that he should exercise a tyrannical control, over his female companion; but treat her on the principle of equality, as a joint associate in the common scenes of life." While his advice on the other duties of husbands and wives had been clear and consistent, when Tullar addressed the issue of husbands' authority and wives' submission he became tangled in a web of contradictions. In one sentence, Tullar proclaimed both that husbands were superior to wives and that husbands should treat wives as joint associates on the principle of equality. At another point in his sermon, Tullar insisted that "not only respect and reverence, but even subjection to husbands is a duty incumbent on wives, as that of an inferior, to a superior." But he also maintained that "wives were never designed for slaves, nor drudges; but to be companions, and partners."[2]

Tullar never acknowledged or resolved the contradiction inherent in his assertion that wives were both submissive inferiors and equal partners. In fact, this tension surrounding the proper relationship between husbands and wives was embedded in early American law and society. Anglo-American custom and law insisted on wives' subordination to their husbands' authority, but it was a subjection that differed significantly from that in other hierarchical relationships. One minister described the nature of wives' subjection as "peculiar . . . not indeed the submission of slaves to their masters, or of subjects to their sov[e]reign, or even of children to a father. —It has more of equality in it—accords with the idea of a helper, companion, friend."[3]

An impressive body of scholarship has analyzed early American wives' legal and economic subordination to their husbands, as well as prescriptive injunctions enjoining wives to be submissive. However, in spite of this legal and cultural consensus, many Americans struggled to define the proper boundaries and character of husbands' authority and wives' submission. Changing marriage ideals that emphasized the importance of love and affection and that rejected the exercise of harsh, authoritative measures complicated this struggle. In the ideal marriage, husbands exercised their authority judiciously and benevolently, while wives offered advice, but submitted willingly and graciously to their husbands' decisions. In the real world, however, wives defied their husbands' authority and men sometimes resorted to violence to enforce their will. Legal treatises, sermons, elopement notices, and divorce petitions reveal that New England men and women disagreed over what separated the legitimate exercise of a husband's authority from illegitimate, unacceptably severe violence. Nor could New Englanders agree on what separated a wife's duty to submit to her husband from her right to escape an intolerably cruel situation. In their desertion postings and divorce petitions, Vermont and Connecticut couples participated in a larger cultural and legal contest over the proper boundaries of patriarchal authority within marriage. Historians have demonstrated that in the early national period, cultural norms increasingly idealized marriage as a companionate union and defined violence within marriage as unacceptable. However, older traditions that identified patriarchal authority as essential to orderly, stable families and communities persisted. Legal ambiguities reflected these cultural tensions, and differences in Connecticut's and Vermont's marriage laws illuminate the contours of this debate as well as the essentially conservative nature of the legal remedies designed to address the abuse of patriarchal power.[4]

On the surface, the cultural consensus throughout the Anglo-American world maintained that "subjection is the portion of the daughters of Eve." Wives heard that they should "read frequently, with due attention, the matrimonial service; and take care, in doing so, not to overlook the word—*obey.*" Prescriptive writers warned that "domestic happiness is disturbed by the attempt of the wife to wear the husband's clothes; or, in other words, by assuming the place of command." Magazine essays counseled wives to "dispute not with [their husbands], let the occasion be what it may; but much rather deny yourself the trifling satisfaction of having your own will." God had decreed wifely submission in the scriptures and Americans agreed that "implicit submission in a man to his wife is ever disgraceful to both; but implicit submission in a wife to the will of her husband is what she promised at the altar: what the good will revere her for, and what is in fact the greatest honour she can receive." Americans believed that wifely submission was vital to the maintenance of stable marriages and families, which in turn provided a secure foundation for an orderly, prosperous society.[5]

Women of the early republic understood the serious consequences of wives' duty to submit to their husbands. Their perceptions of the dependent, subordinate status of wives caused many single women to experience what historian Nancy Cott has termed "marriage trauma," a reluctance ever to marry or an emotional withdrawal from the marriage relationship.[6] These young women recognized that "care should be taken not to relinquish the ease, and independence of a single life, to become the slave of a fool, or a tyrant's caprice." Women knew that they would be required to submit to their husbands, but they also knew that the nature of that submission would differ according to whether their husbands were fools, tyrants, or men who expected "a reasonable and advantageous submission," men to whom their wives could be "submissive from choice, and obedient from inclination."[7] A young woman had to take great care in choosing her future husband, for their marriage would place her under his authority. Because divorce in many states was difficult, if not impossible, the choice of a marriage partner had life-long implications. Not all women chose well. In her retort to her husband's elopement notice, Esther Kimball detailed his abuse and lack of support, and then stated, "I write this to let people know that if I was foolish for marrying you that your ill usage has learnt me some wit." A woman's foolish choice could result in a marriage plagued by quarreling, abuse, or poverty. Esther Kimball realized her mistake too late: she remained estranged from her husband and died a pauper in 1859.[8]

Ministers and the authors of a vast body of prescriptive literature repeatedly emphasized wives' obligation to submit to their husbands; however, a closer examination of this surface consensus reveals contradictions and tensions regarding husbands' authority and wives' submission. Writers often blamed the tyranny of husbands for marital difficulties. They repeatedly reminded husbands that "God has not required from the woman the submission of a slave." One newspaper essayist explained that when a husband will "use a woman of sense, birth, and fortune, every way equal to himself, as a slave or a fool, it is no wonder that domestic peace is interrupted." In *The Guide to Domestic Happiness,* William Giles advised husbands not "to impose what is unreasonable" or "to enforce any thing but what conscience demonstrates to be right, and urges as a duty." Prescriptive authors agreed that wifely submission was not slavery and that husbands should not be unreasonable tyrants, but they had difficulty translating these broad precepts into prescriptions for everyday life. One minister declared that if husbands "let conjugal authority be founded upon love, be never exercised in opposition to revelation or reason, and be regulated by the idea of companionship, . . . then there needs no particular rules for its guidance." Most ministers and authors were not satisfied with such vague maxims, however, and many sought to outline the nature and boundaries of wives' submission in more precise terms. Their advice, as well as evidence from desertion notices, demonstrates that a wife's duty to submit frequently clashed with a reality in which it was not always possible or desirable for women to defer to their husbands.[9]

Ministers placed one limitation upon wifely submission without hesitation: wives must not submit to their husbands if in doing so they would disobey God. One pastor warned wives that "if the demands of a husband oppose the will of God, you are pre-engaged by a law of universal operation, and 'ought to obey GOD rather than man.'" The anonymous author of *The Wife* explained, "I would not here be understood that a woman should yield a slavish submission to every little whim or caprice of her husband; or to relinquish her reason and judgment to gratify his folly: no, that might be, perhaps, to sin against a more supreme authority than what the law has conferred on him." These writers advised women to judge the requests and commands of their husbands and to use their reason to determine whether obeying their husbands would violate God's laws.[10]

The Puritan doctrine of the equality of all souls made women accountable before God for their own actions and salvation. Did wives' accountability before God supersede their accountability to their husbands? Two Vermont women demonstrated the extremes to which ministerial advice to "obey God rather than man" might be taken. Both Zebulon Huntington and Ammi Andrews reported in their desertion postings that their wives had left them to join the Shakers, a religious order that abolished marriage, practiced celibacy, and advocated greater equality between men and women. Mary Andrews and Hannah Huntington defied their husbands' authority by joining the Shakers, but they no doubt believed it was God's will for them to do so. When ministers and essayists counseled wives to obey God they did not intend their remarks to support women who left husbands and possibly children to join religious sects that espoused radical doctrines proclaiming equality between men and women. However, their comments contributed to a confusion about married women's relationship to God that stretched back to Ann Hutchinson, Sarah Osborne, and other colonial women who dared to claim that following God's will released them from traditional gender roles.[11]

Wives' desire to obey God did not disrupt most marriages to the extent that it did the Huntingtons and Andrewses. Yet sermons and marriage manuals offered other advice that revealed some tensions surrounding wives' roles in more practical, day-to-day settings. When Hannah Loomis of Montpelier, Vermont, died in December 1813, Reverend Chester Wright commiserated,

> Let us weep with a husband . . . [who] had hoped with her to pass the remainder of his days; to enjoy her assistance in the cares and duties of domestic life; to share with her every pleasure; to divide with her the weight of every trouble; to receive her advice in every emergency, and to have his virtue strengthened by her prudent and discreet example.

This picture of Hannah Loomis shows her assisting, advising, strengthening, dividing, and sharing with her husband. Reverend Wright did not commend Hannah for her submissive qualities; rather, he praised her as a partner and an advisor. Likewise, Reverend Asa Burton praised Joanna Shaw because "the trials of her husband she alleviated by her counsels," and Reverend Isaiah Parker expressed his sorrow for Esther Chaplin's husband, who had lost "the partner of your joys and sorrows . . . in whose good judgment, fidelity and integrity you could place the greatest confidence—one with whom you took sweet counsel." Funeral sermons for married women frequently extolled wives for having been model partners, for having shared equally in the cares and concerns of their families, and for having advised their husbands on family affairs.[12]

The model of the wife as partner, and especially as an advisor, was a popular one in prescriptive literature. Advice authors told husbands to "deliberate with her who ought to be his dearest, and is his most disinterested friend—even in those affairs which it is his immediate duty to superintend. He may derive useful hints from a female mind." The husband also "should consult his wife on money matters generally, not only because she is also interested, but her advice may be a saving of much expense . . . believe me, however confident you may be of your sufficiency to judge of the disposal of your case, you will receive great benefit by such consultations." Instead of describing wives' roles in submissive, deferential terms, these authors portrayed married women as capable advisors and active partners in the management of family affairs.[13]

Authors and ministers did not believe that this model of wife-as-partner/advisor conflicted with the model of wife-as-submissive-subordinate. Instead, they believed the two models were entirely compatible. The good wife offered her husband advice, but she let him make the ultimate decisions and then helped him carry out those decisions, even if she disagreed with them. A wife was a junior partner in the family enterprise: she should "be made acquainted with . . . and give her opinion in relation to the management and disposal of" family affairs; however, "This privilege should always be taken with the utmost caution and discretion, and never exerted, or too strenuously enforced." A wife could advise her husband on the proper course of action to take in the family's interest, but "whenever she attempts to create an interest of her own separate from the interest of her husband; or to establish for herself a reputation independent of his, she is assuming a character which does not belong to her . . . [and is] laying a sure foundation for domestic wretchedness and strife." If a husband and wife disagreed over what course of action to take, the wife had to submit to her husband's decisions. Prescriptive writers believed that the opportunity to offer their opinions compensated for the submission that was then required of wives. One essayist claimed that "would [the husband] consult her on his affairs, converse with her freely upon all subjects . . . she would rattle the marriage chains with less impatience and difficulty." Wives had to content themselves with their advisory role and not attempt to usurp their husbands' decision-making authority.[14]

Likewise, prescriptive writers were quick to praise the beneficial effects of women's influence on their husbands, but careful to remind wives that their influence over men should not extend to control. These authors celebrated women's ability to turn men away from vice and toward virtue while warning wives to "avoid all thoughts of managing a husband." In a newspaper essay entitled "Female Influence," the author praised women for being

> of great service to mankind. Many young men have by their [women's] virtuous example been allured from the apparently blooming paths of vicious pleasure, into the road of virtue leading to happiness. For their sake, the drunkard hath relinquished his cup, the gamester his table, the profane swearer his blasphemous imprecations, and even the debauchee has sometimes returned to continence. By their influence, sloth has been metamorphosed into diligence, pride and arrogance, into modesty and affability, and cowardice itself into bravery.

Male authors believed that women were capable of turning vicious men into virtuous citizens, but they were never completely comfortable with the power of women's influence. They quickly added that, while "a virtuous woman is the glory of human nature, a female, without prudence, is a very dangerous character." Women were both "the source of good and evil to man," capable of reforming vicious husbands but also capable of "destroying the harmony and tranquility of families" by attempting to exert so much influence that they challenged their husbands' authority.[15]

Most prescriptive writers dealt with the issue of women's influence as they had handled wives' role as advisors: women could attempt to influence their husbands, but ultimately they had to submit. One minister advised wives who were "united with a man of . . . dishonorable habits, or vicious practices," that an "affectionate and dignified course of conduct

. . . [would] succeed in reclaiming him from vice, and restoring him to virtue." However, should these "laudable exertions fail, and should poverty and distress be, finally, the unhappy consequence of your union with such a man, you will enjoy the rich satisfaction of having faithfully performed your duty." If wives could not persuade their husbands to live virtuously, they had to suffer the consequences. Female submission was necessary because "order and peace in any community . . . require that those of every rank should be respected according to their rank. The want of this, is invariably attended with disorder and confusion." To avoid this disorder and confusion in the family, Reverend Martin Tullar advised husbands to "take the lead of all family concerns. It belongs to them to administer family government. . . . In this little republic, the husband is a principle, the wife a secondary officer." In an era when egalitarian, democratic ideals were replacing deferential political traditions, many authors sought to bolster the family as a bastion of hierarchy. They believed that a wife could attempt to exercise her influence, but in the end she was a "secondary officer" who owed deference and subjection to her superior officer, her husband.[16]

This cultural consensus in favor of wives' submission to their husbands complemented a legal system in which wives' subordination was firmly entrenched. However, while the common law clearly established wives' subordination, it was subject to differing interpretations that highlighted tensions regarding husbands' authority and wifely submission. Coverture, which incorporated a woman's legal existence into that of her husband, neatly meshed wives' legal and economic subordination: because they had no separate legal existence, married women could not own property or their own wages, could not enter into contracts, and could not sue or be sued. These legal prohibitions barred wives from most independent action in the economic arena. Like servants and minor children, wives legally were dependent on male household heads for economic support, and in return owed service and obedience. In his *Commentaries on American Law*, James Kent explained that "as the husband is the guardian of the wife, and bound to protect and maintain her, the law has given him a reasonable superiority and control over her person." The words "child" or "servant" could be substituted for "wife" and this statement would retain its legal validity in the early national period.[17]

In spite of the similarities among the legal positions of wives, servants, and children, the law recognized that the relationship between husbands and wives was a more equal one than that between parent and child or master and servant. James Kent granted that the husband had a certain amount of control over his wife. However, in *The Law of Baron and Feme*, a detailed discourse on the relationship between husbands and wives, the Connecticut jurist Tapping Reeve presented a more ambiguous picture:

> I apprehend it will be found difficult to ascertain, with exactness, what power the husband has over the person of his wife. According to the ideas once entertained upon the subject . . . the husband seems to have had the same right over the person of his wife that he had over the person of his apprentice: to chastise her moderately or confine her. . . . [In more recent times] wives began to receive a more liberal treatment. Their rights were better understood than heretofore. They assumed more the character of companions than of servants to their husbands.

Reeve went on to say that "the increased refinements of modern times" prevented the law from recognizing a husband's right to chastise his wife as he could his servant. In fact, he asserted that the law recognized wives' right to leave their husbands when they were subjected to cruel treatment: "the court will never take away a wife from a friend to whom she has fled to escape the effects of his [her husband's] brutality, and order her to be delivered to her husband."[18]

But what constituted treatment cruel enough to justify a court's recognition of a wife's right to leave her husband? Reeve left this question unanswered, but other jurists clearly defined cruelty in narrow terms. In his *Digest of the Laws of the State of Connecticut*, Zephaniah Swift expressed his belief that it was "unreasonable and unjust" to expect a wife to perform her duties *only* if her husband had "treated her with extreme cruelty, and . . . by personal abuse, endangered her life." James Kent was even more specific on this issue than Swift; according to Kent, in order for the law to consider a husband's actions as intolerably severe,

> the causes must be grave and weighty, and show such a state of personal danger as that the duties of the married life cannot be discharged. Mere austerity of temper, petulance of manners, rudeness of language, a want of civil attention, even occasional sallies of passion, if they do not threaten bodily harm, do not amount to that cruelty against which the law can relieve. The wife must disarm such a disposition in the husband by the weapons of kindness.

Swift and Kent feared that allowing separations or divorces on the grounds of cruelty had the potential to disrupt marital patriarchy. Permitting wives to leave their husbands because of cruel treatment implied that it was appropriate for women to judge their husbands' behavior and to take steps to remove themselves from their husbands' control if they believed that their husbands had acted in an unacceptably severe manner. Their desire to preserve husbands' authority led jurists such as Swift and Kent to limit the definition of intolerably severe behavior to actions that caused bodily harm and endangered women's lives.[19]

In their elopement notices, Connecticut and Vermont husbands demonstrated a similar concern with maintaining their authority within their marriages. These husbands acted on Swift's declaration that the "husband has power and dominion over his wife . . . he may control, regulate and restrain her conduct, and keep her by force within the bounds of duty, and under due subjection and subordination." Husbands intended their newspaper postings to "control, regulate and restrain" their wives' behavior by denying the women access to their credit. The language of many husbands' notices demonstrates the men's assumption that they were entitled to obedience from their wives and that they were entitled to take steps to control their wives' behavior when they believed their wives had disobeyed. Many men echoed the husband who accused his wife of acting "without my advice or consent" and the husband who claimed that his wife had "disobeyed my lawful commands." Husbands lamented that their wives were "disobedient, clamorous," and "not willing to be restrained." Jeremiah Perrin claimed that his wife "refused to comply with my reasonable requests." These husbands and wives could not agree on the proper boundaries of husbands' authority and wives' submission. The requests that Jeremiah Perrin believed were reasonable apparently seemed tyrannical or capricious to his wife, Hannah.[20]

Husbands who published desertion notices believed that when their wives' obedience was not forthcoming, they had no obligation to carry out their duties, and removed their financial protection from their wives. By refusing to pay their wives' debts, husbands highlighted married women's economic dependence and subordinate status. Husbands often emphasized their superior status within the marriage relationship, as did Henry Gould in his January 1817 notice: "Whereas my wife, Betsey, has against my inclination, eloped to parts unknown, and has otherwise violated the solemn duties of the marriage covenant, I do, therefore, forbid all persons from harboring, trusting, or entertaining this despoiler of my house and fugitive from my bed, as the contrary thereof shall be answered according to law." Gould's language is very patriarchal: his wife acted against *his* inclination, despoiled *his* house, and ran away from *his* bed. Gould would have understood Abraham Holmes's complaint that his wife Judah had "left my house without any just provocation, and refuses to take her place in my family." Holmes asserted the right to determine his wife's proper place in *his* family. Gould and Holmes thought of their marriages in terms of hierarchies and duties. They believed that the marriage covenant gave them authority to lay claim to their wives' obedience. When that obedience was not forthcoming, they felt no obligation to carry out their duties and removed their financial protection from their wives. Husbands could carry this patriarchal stance to an extreme, as did Samuel Bigelow, who not only refused to pay his eloped wife's debts but also forbade "any man or men lodging with her for the future, as she is my property." Although Bigelow was the only New England husband in this study who explicitly claimed that his wife was his property, his notice is an extreme example of the power that husbands could attempt to exercise over their subordinate wives.[21]

Husbands also revealed their assumptions regarding their right to control their wives' behavior when they included terms of reconciliation in their newspaper postings. After announcing his wife Soviah's desertion, John Miller declared that "if she will return to her duty . . . and behave well, she shall be well used." Husbands used desertion notices to pressure their wives to return, submit, and obey. These husbands admitted that they wanted and even needed their wives to return, but only if the women renewed their obedience. When reconciliations did occur, husbands occasionally placed notices announcing that they would resume paying their wives' debts. Even on these occasions, husbands' desire for authority over their wives was evident. After Parker and Mercy Chapy reconciled, he printed a notice in which he claimed to be "heartily sorry" for originally advertising that she had "refused to obey my lawful commands." He then added that "it is my desire to wipe off the stain, and that her character may be considered on . . . good terms." In his first advertisement, Chapy had laid claim to his wife's obedience; in his second he claimed control over her reputation.[22]

A desertion notice did more than discontinue a man's financial obligations toward his wife; it also threatened to destroy a woman's place in the community by maligning her character. When a husband printed an elopement notice, he was making public his judgment that his wife had not fulfilled her marital responsibilities and duties. If a woman was a good wife, she was a valued, respected member of her community. But a woman who disregarded her marital duties failed at the primary role her community expected of her. Aware of these expectations, husbands attempted to use postings to shape their communities' perceptions of their wives. Husbands who convinced the people of their communities that their wives had behaved improperly could be sure that their neighbors would apply a good deal of social pressure to persuade their wives to return and behave as they should. Like Parker Chapy, husbands who published desertion postings claimed the right to publicly judge whether or not their wives were sufficiently submissive, and they expected their communities to abide by their judgments.

The wives that these men described as unsubmissive and disobedient measured their own and their husbands' behavior by different standards. When wives responded to their husbands' notices, they did not challenge the ideal of wifely submission, but declared that their husbands' demands and treatment were unreasonable. After proclaiming herself "a true and faithful wife," Abigail Pell explained that she had left her husband James because "instead of being treated as a wife ought to be, [she] was treated worse than a slave." Pell did not deny that she owed her husband obedience; instead, she claimed to have been a faithful wife. She objected to being treated in a way that denied that her status as a wife entitled her to more than abject servitude. She believed that her husband had abused his authority over her, but she did not challenge his right to exercise that authority, provided that he did so properly and judiciously. Other women's notices reveal that what they objected to was not their husbands' authority over them, but the violent manner in which their husbands attempted to exercise that authority. Chloe Ames reported that if she "did not comply with [her husband's commands] then [he] threatens beatings and turning out of doors." Betsey Lewis explicitly and sarcastically drew a connection between her husband's abuse and issues of authority and obedience in her notice: "I left his person after being severely treated, and repeatedly told by him to go, for if I did not, he would make me go—and we are commanded to obey our husbands. I therefore, like an obedient wife obeyed him." Lewis managed to portray herself as an obedient wife while she drew attention to the injustice of conventions that demanded wifely submission in the face of husbands' brutality.[23]

Both Vermont and Connecticut wives complained of their husbands' cruelty in their postings; however, Connecticut wives were far less likely to do so than their Vermont counterparts. While cruelty accusations appear in 47 percent of Vermont women's postings, only 20 percent of Connecticut wives who posted notices complained of such behavior. Given that the content of Connecticut and Vermont women's notices is otherwise statistically similar, this one difference is striking. Not coincidentally, this discrepancy reflects an important difference between Vermont's and Connecticut's divorce laws and procedures, a difference that helps illuminate cultural ambiguities regarding the proper exercise of patriarchal authority within marriage.[24]

Connecticut's divorce statute dated from the seventeenth century, and remained unchanged until 1846. The Connecticut colonial assembly gave the superior court the authority to grant divorces on the grounds of fraudulent contract, adultery, willful desertion for three years, or seven years' absence with no communication, in which case the absent party was considered legally dead.[25] In 1779, Vermont adopted the Connecticut statute word for word. However, in 1787 the Vermont legislature added intolerable severity to the list of grounds for which the state supreme court could grant divorces, and in 1805 it added impotence, making the Vermont law one of the most lenient in the nation at that time. Between 1790 and 1830, 48 percent of Vermont wives who asked the court for divorce included the accusation of intolerable severity in their petitions. Because the Vermont Supreme Court applied the divorce law liberally, denying only five of 259 petitions presented in Chittenden, Washington, and Windsor counties between 1790 and 1830, legitimizing intolerable severity as grounds for divorce appears to have enabled significant numbers of Vermont women to escape abusive marriages.[26] Connecticut women married to violent husbands were not entirely without means of relief. Although the superior court could not grant divorces for cruelty, the Connecticut Assembly could and did grant legislative decrees dissolving marriages because of husbands' abusive treatment. Between 1789 and 1819, 71 percent of women who petitioned the assembly for divorce due to their husbands' cruelty were successful.[27]

The requirement that Connecticut women petition the state legislature for divorce on the grounds of cruelty—an intimidating and expensive process—as well as the somewhat lower success rate of those who did so suggest that Connecticut women experiencing domestic abuse did not receive as sympathetic a hearing as did Vermont wives in similar situations. This important difference may help explain why Vermont wives more frequently accused their spouses of cruelty in their newspaper notices. In

Vermont, a cruelty accusation carried greater legal legitimacy than did the same accusation in Connecticut. Connecticut and Vermont appear to have arrived at different conclusions regarding the appropriate boundaries of husbands' authority, with the Connecticut legislature feeling the need to scrutinize cruelty cases closely to ensure the preservation of traditional marital hierarchy.[28] However, in spite of these significant legal and procedural differences, a closer look at divorce practice in each state reveals striking similarities that demonstrate the ambiguous nature of laws that allowed wives to challenge their husbands' authority.

All divorce petitions forced the Vermont and Connecticut courts, as well as the Connecticut Assembly, to confront the ambiguities of the common law marriage contract. Judges and legislators had to weigh the rights and responsibilities of husbands and wives and determine whether one party had violated the rights of the other to such an extent that the marriage should be dissolved. Wives called upon the courts and the legislature to make this decision far more frequently than did husbands. Vermont women presented 72 percent of all divorce petitions to the state supreme court and Connecticut wives initiated 76 percent of the divorce petitions that appeared before that state's superior court. Connecticut women also presented 78 percent of divorce petitions to the state assembly.[29] Scholars often consider access to divorce to be an important marker of women's rights and status; however, the fact that wives more than husbands turned to the courts or legislature to resolve their marital difficulties also points to women's disadvantageous position within the marriage relationship. Husbands could resolve problems with their wives by exerting their authority in more informal ways. Husbands' ability to deny their wives credit often granted them sufficient power to persuade their wives to act as they wished. Wives did not have as much power within the marriage relationship and therefore appealed to the authority of the courts and state assemblies to resolve their difficulties.[30]

The willingness of courts and legislatures to grant divorces on the grounds of cruelty did not stem from their recognition of wives' equal rights. Rather, judges and legislators granted such divorces because they recognized women's relative weakness within the marriage relationship. Arguments in favor of divorce on the grounds of intolerable severity never questioned the basic tenets of patriarchal marriage. Instead, divorce proponents acknowledged the inevitability of male authority and female submission within marriage and insisted that divorce was necessary to deal with abuses that occurred within that inevitable hierarchy. One article, "On Divorce," which appeared in Philadelphia's *National Recorder* in 1819 made just such an argument. The author believed that divorce on the grounds of cruelty was needed because marriage

> imposes a yoke for life upon two unequal beings, the one of whom has in his favor strength and authority, which he may abuse against the weakness of the other. . . . Ought not the unfortunate victim to be lamented and sucored [sic], who instead of finding a friend in a husband, finds only an odious tyrant; whose angry transports threaten her life; or who, by a slow and meditated cruelty, makes of her life a torture more frightful than death?

Divorce proponents did not intend divorce on the grounds of intolerable severity to threaten *all* husbands' authority; rather, divorce made that authority more palatable by providing a way to deal with abuses.[31]

Even Vermont wives—who enjoyed a 99 percent success rate when petitioning the supreme court for divorce—recognized the limited nature of the power the divorce statute granted them. Of the eighty-nine women who accused their husbands of cruelty in their divorce petitions, twenty-six petitioned for divorce on the *sole* grounds of intolerable severity, a total of only fourteen percent of *all* women's petitions. The great majority of women did not believe that the single charge of intolerable severity was sufficient grounds for the court to remove them permanently from their husbands' control. These women also included charges of desertion or adultery (or both) in their petitions. Many women who charged their husbands with cruelty carefully documented the specific actions their husbands had taken, as well as the date and location of the incidents. In 1813, Phebe Huston of Burlington petitioned for a divorce from her husband Thomas on the grounds of intolerable severity and desertion. Her charges were quite specific. Huston claimed that on July 10, 1809, "the sd [sic] Thomas at a place called Caldwell's Manor . . . treated the petitioner with intolerable severity, by whipping, kicking and turning her out of his house and hath ever since refused to live with or provid[e] for her." Women such as Phebe Huston understood that the courts would not deprive a husband of his authority over his wife without specific, incontrovertible proof of cruelty.[32]

Vermont women who wrote desertion notices often equated intolerable severity with such mental cruelty as threats and insults. Esther Woodbury claimed that it was her husband's "ill treatment and hard threatenings that drove me from his house" while Anna Norris accused her husband of abuse because "[w]hen we lived together, you have wished me back to my fathers—said I could not go too quick nor stay too long; you have wished me dead, and you have wished me in hell." Although many women believed such treatment justified leaving their husbands, Vermont wives recognized that the courts interpreted intolerable severity narrowly and most women who charged their husbands with cruelty in their divorce petitions only referred to violent physical abuse. In her 1805 divorce petition, Rachel Nichols charged that her husband Joseph "often threatened to take away her life with heated Tongs & other like deadly Weapons; that he used frequently to whip her, with large and unreasonable whips & weapons, and to torture her by punishing and other means." Nichols's use of the word "unreasonable" is telling: did she fear that the court believed that a certain amount of physical force on the husband's part when disciplining his wife was reasonable? Her petition suggests that Nichols recognized she needed to convince the court that her husband's use of force went beyond the boundaries of what was reasonable. The women who petitioned for divorce on the grounds of intolerable severity knew that they were challenging their husbands' rightful authority over them. Their petitions reveal that they understood that in order to convince the court to remove them from their husbands' authority, they had to prove—in James Kent's words—that the causes were "grave and weighty."[33]

Wives who petitioned the Connecticut Assembly for divorce on the grounds of cruelty also faced a strict standard of proof. Connecticut women who petitioned on the grounds of cruelty alone were less likely to be successful than were those women who combined an accusation of cruelty with adultery, desertion, or nonsupport. When women petitioned on the sole grounds of cruelty, they received divorce decrees 69 percent of the time. In contrast, pairing cruelty with another accusation raised Connecticut wives' success rate to 82 percent. Connecticut records indicate that the assembly was unwilling to grant divorce decrees without clear evidence of violent physical abuse. For example, in April 1796, Ruth Shelton of Woodbury petitioned the assembly for a divorce because her husband William had treated her "in a savage & cruel manner & refused to provide her with a physician or proper attendance or medicine during illness." Shelton's petition was accompanied by six depositions testifying to "neglect by William Shelton during illness of his wife." Ruth Shelton believed that her husband's failure to provide her with proper medical care was savage and cruel and warranted a divorce decree. The assembly, however, disagreed and voted against granting her petition. The assembly records do not contain an explanation of the legislators' reasoning; however, the Connecticut lawmakers clearly did not believe that William Shelton's neglect of his wife during her illness met the high standard required to prove intolerable severity. The legislature only granted divorces for severe, physical abuse, such as that detailed by Eunice Bird in her petition. Bird claimed that her husband John had committed acts of "personal violence such as striking kicking & dragging her about the house forcing her cloaths from her back & commiting them to the flames and frequently threatened her life." Uncomfortable with granting women the right to judge whether their husbands exercised authority appropriately, the Connecticut legislature tried to ensure that they removed wives from their husbands' control only when the women were in serious physical danger.[34]

In addition to meeting strict standards of proof, Vermont and Connecticut women also framed their divorce petitions to present themselves as obedient, submissive wives. Those women who asked for divorce on the grounds of cruelty did not question the propriety of patriarchal authority within marriage; rather, they challenged the abuse of that authority. Ruby Gleason's claim that she had "lived in the faithful and affectionate performance of the duties enjoined by the marriage covenant" appeared in almost every woman's divorce petition. Wives seeking divorce were careful to present themselves as the blameless victims of their husbands' abuse. When Sarah Arnold petitioned the Connecticut Assembly for divorce in 1803, she catalogued examples of her husband Asa's violent acts toward her, and then added that "she find[s] soothing expressions of no avail" in deterring his abuse. Women such as Arnold knew that in order to receive a sympathetic hearing, they had to convince the courts or legislature that they accepted their inferior position within the marriage relationship, and that, rather than give their spouses any reason to find fault with them, they had done all in their power to please their husbands.[35] Connecticut and Vermont women acknowledged that they needed protection because they were the weaker, subordinate party in the marriage relationship. In her divorce petition, Vermonter Rebecca Newell claimed that her husband William "did beat, bruise, & wound, in a most cruel manner your petitioner and while she was sick and most in need of his friendly care and assistance." Newell presented herself as weak and sickly, in need of assistance from her stronger husband. However, instead of finding the care and concern that an obedient dependent subordinate expected to receive from a superior, Newell found abuse and violent treatment. She appealed to the court for protection because she received no protection from her husband.[36]

The emphasis on wives' weakness and subordination to their husbands in divorce proponents' arguments and in women's own divorce petitions helps reveal the ambiguities surrounding the practice of granting divorces on the grounds of intolerable severity, as well as the difficulties New England men and women faced as they struggled to determine the acceptable limits of husbands' authority and wives' submission. The image of the weak, dependent wife was crucial to New Englanders' attempts to negotiate between newer ideals emphasizing companionship within marriage and older patriarchal traditions. The continuing acceptance of wifely submission helped make it possible for norms that valued love and affection within marriage and that presented husbands and wives as partners to co-exist with traditions and a legal system that supported husbands' ultimate authority. In the ideal marriage, husbands loved their wives and never asked them to do anything unreasonable. Husbands accepted their spouses' advice; however, they also expected their wives' submission. If conflict occurred, wives, as the weaker, subordinate spouse, were expected to defer to their husbands' decisions. If, in spite of the women's deference, conflict persisted and turned violent, wives (again, as the weaker, subordinate spouse) were entitled to protection.

Because they were able to petition for divorce on the grounds of cruelty, wives in Connecticut and Vermont had access to an important form of relief that was not available to women in all other states. Granting divorces because of husbands' cruel treatment suggests that early national judges and legislators were willing to limit husbands' authority over their wives and that they were willing to allow wives to judge their husbands' exercise of authority. But that willingness was predicated on a restricted definition of cruelty and on the acceptance of wives' inferior position within marriage. Women's elopement notices reveal that they believed threats, neglect, and mental cruelty to be unacceptable manifestations of their husbands' authority, but the Vermont courts and Connecticut Assembly only accepted physical violence as sufficient justification for removing a wife from her husband's control.

The New England wives who sought divorce because of their husbands' abusive treatment understood that, paradoxically, it was their dependent, subordinate status that allowed them to escape from their husbands' authority. Wives' subordinate position placed them firmly under their husbands' authority, as husbands' attempts to compel their wives' obedience by withdrawing the women's access to their credit illustrate. Yet, the power that husbands wielded over wives entitled married women to protection against cruel, abusive treatment. While New England women forcefully defended their rights in their desertion notices and divorce petitions, married women were careful to present themselves as faithful wives who had fulfilled their marital obligations. Wives could claim their rights only if they behaved in ways that affirmed their status as the weaker, dependent spouse. Hundreds of desertion notices and divorce petitions served to notify New England couples that they were not alone as they struggled to determine where husbands' authority ended and wives' rights began.

2

"A Trifling Sum"

Economic Support and Consumer
Spending in New England Marriages

On October 11, 1813, Uriah Hayes of Sharon, Vermont, placed an advertisement in the *Vermont Republican*:

> Whereas Rachel my wife has for reasons unknown to me but better known to herself, Eloped from me, and I had rather see the delicacy of the Cheek and hand tarnished with labor to procure subsistence than any other way; therefore I forbid all persons harboring or trusting her on my account, for I shall pay no debts of her contracting after this date.

Uriah and Rachel Hayes had been married ten years when Rachel deserted; within one year of this notice's publication, the couple had reconciled. They lived together for several more years and registered the birth of a daughter, Rachel, in 1817. However, in February of 1819, Rachel sued Uriah for divorce, claiming that his intolerable severity had driven both her and their daughter out of his home in November 1818. The Vermont Supreme Court granted Rachel the divorce and ordered Uriah to pay her 150 dollars a year in alimony for the rest of her life. In spite of the court order, Uriah refused to pay the alimony, and in 1823 Rachel sued him for six hundred dollars. The Windsor County Court upheld Rachel's claim; however, because Uriah had relocated to Boston and was not present at the trial, Rachel received no part of the cash award. Instead, she received part of the farm that Uriah still owned in Sharon. The land records do not reveal the acreage of her portion, but the plot contained a saw mill, some land in cultivation, and a house. Although the court intended that this land support Rachel Hayes during her life, court and land records reveal that she experienced financial difficulties. Rachel appeared in Windsor County Court on debt charges in 1824, and to obtain cash, she leased small plots of her land over the next several years. In 1829, she sold her lifetime interest in the land to her son Allen for one hundred dollars and the right to continue to live in part of the house and to maintain a small garden plot. Rachel lived with her son until her death at age fifty-four in 1841.[1]

The story of Rachel and Uriah Hayes demonstrates many of the ambiguities surrounding marital and gender relations in the early national period. Uriah's notice denying Rachel access to his credit reveals the tremendous power men wielded over their wives as a result of married women's legal and economic dependence. Rachel and Uriah may have reconciled in part because of the difficulties that Rachel faced supporting herself apart from her husband. However, Rachel was able to obtain a divorce and an alimony award, testimony to the Vermont Court's support for a woman's right to leave a cruel husband and to receive adequate economic support. Yet Rachel's legal victory had mixed results. Uriah was able to avoid two court orders to pay Rachel, and although the court's land award enabled her to live independently for a time, after ten years of struggling to support herself, Rachel only achieved economic security by becoming a dependent in her son's household.

Desertion notices, divorce petitions, and other court records dealing with marital strife demonstrate that the limitations wives of the early republic faced and the opportunities they pursued were inextricably linked. *Feme covert* status burdened married women with tremendous legal disabilities. According to the common law, wives were economically dependent on their husbands and were subject to their husbands' authority. With few exceptions, the law denied married women the right to independent action in the legal and economic arenas. However, their status as dependent subordinates also guaranteed wives certain rights. Because they could not act as independent economic agents, the common law recognized wives' right to adequate economic support from their husbands. The records that estranged couples left behind reveal the tensions that existed between husbands' legal and economic power as heads of households and their wives' right to support. These tensions played themselves out over such issues as living arrangements, consumer spending, and debt, and they reveal much about the ways in which husbands and wives responded to developments that were transforming New England's economy. While husbands held tremendous legal and economic power over their wives, the experiences of married couples demonstrate that wives were able to pursue their own interests, within limits. Marriage was an unequal bargain; the rights of wives did not alter the imbalance of power favoring husbands in the traditional marriage relationship. The opportunities that wives pursued to defend their interests and rights rested upon the very disabilities that limited their options.[2]

As with Uriah Hayes, husbands' most immediate reason for placing elopement notices was to absolve themselves from any responsibility for their wives' support. Because a husband received control of his wife's property, wages, and labor, the common law required him to "provide his wife with necessaries suitable to her situation and his condition in life; and if she contracts debt due for them . . . he is obliged to pay those debts." However, the common law recognized one exception to this obligation: in his *Commentaries on the Laws of England,* William Blackstone wrote, "if a wife elopes . . . the husband is not chargeable even for necessaries, at least if the person who furnishes them is sufficiently apprized [sic] of the elopement." Husbands used newspaper notices to inform merchants and artisans that their financial obligations toward their wives had ceased because the women had deserted.[3]

Husbands used desertion postings to reassert their legal authority over their wives. According to common law traditions, husbands' authority was considerable, extending to their wives' spending habits and living arrangements. Wives were entitled to economic support only if they obeyed their husbands, an obligation that included living in a place of their husbands' choosing. In his treatise on the common law in America, James Kent explained that if a husband "shifts his domicile, the wife is bound to follow him wherever he chooses to go." A wife who did not follow her husband when he moved was legally considered to have deserted him and thereby lost her right to his support. Richard Hills denied his wife credit because she "refuses to live with me at such a place as I think best." In 1801, Rufus Baldwin refused his wife access to his credit because he was "about to move into a distant part of the country" and his wife was "not willing to go with me." Husbands also could arrange for their wives to live apart from them without relinquishing control of their spouses' behavior. Jesse Moon denied his wife credit because he had "provided for [her] a home abroad, where she has lived till a few days since, but now refuses to live at that place or to return and live with me." The fact that the Moons had separated did not relieve Jesse of his duty to pro-

vide for his wife; nor did the separation deprive him of his legal authority over his spouse. Husbands did not hesitate to use that authority to
deny their wives credit when the women disobeyed their wishes.[4]

Courts regularly upheld husbands' right to deny support to wives who
refused to live where the men chose. In 1796 the Connecticut Superior
Court denied Frances Sistare's application for dower because she had refused to leave her native Spain to join her husband Gabriel when he
moved to New London. Frances argued that their separation was due to
her husband's adulterous relationship with another woman: "Gabriel
having soon after his arrival at said New London, taken to his bed and
board another woman, with whom he lived until his death, and by whom
he had several children . . . said Frances remaining in Spain absent from
said Gabriel, was through his default and not hers." From the court's perspective, Gabriel's adultery was irrelevant; the important issue was
Frances choosing to remain apart from her husband. In spite of the fact
that he had left her to reside in New London, Frances's "remaining absent from her husband in a foreign country against his consent" disqual-
ified her from receiving a portion of her husband's estate. Legally, by not
following her husband, Frances Sistare had deserted. She had defied
Gabriel's authority to determine where the couple would live and, therefore, forfeited any claim she might have had to a share of his estate.[5]

The law clearly favored husbands in disputes over where to live. However, the content of desertion postings indicates that such disputes did not
generate conflict to the extent that wives' spending habits did. Many New
England men echoed William Hector, who complained that his wife ran
him into debt "far beyond my ability to pay." The claim that their wives
were incurring unreasonable debts was the second most common complaint to appear in both Connecticut and Vermont husbands' notices.
These men wanted to regain control of their wives' consumer activities,
which they claimed threatened to ruin them financially. In 1795, Thomas
Sloan claimed that his wife Susanna had "run me in debt to the amount of
Two Hundred and Eighty-four Pounds Nineteen Shillings and Nine Pence,
at the Store of *Michael & Thomas Bull,* in the city of Hartford, for which
sum an attachment was laid on my House and Lot of Land." Over thirty
years later, in 1827, Nathan Kinne accused his wife Elizabeth of being "in
an unjustifiable habit for a number of years of trading and running me in
debt at the stores." Because wives had no credit of their own, their husbands could use newspaper advertisements to control the women's access
to the marketplace and to curtail their consumer activities.[6]

However, married women were not powerless. Their notices reveal a strong sense of the rights the common law granted to wives and indicate that married women were willing to act to protect those rights. Women recognized that the common law offered protection to wives who had not deserted but whose husbands had denied them credit. Common law traditions allowed men to prohibit their wives' purchasing luxuries, but husbands could not withdraw their wives' access to their credit for *all* purchases. James Kent explained that unless she eloped, "the husband cannot deprive the wife of the liberty which the law gives her of providing necessaries at his expense for her preservation." Approximately one-third of New England wives who responded to their husbands' accusations denied that they had deserted. Sally Meigs asked a series of rhetorical questions in her response to her husband's notice: "Have I eloped from his bed . . . ? Have I been inconstant? Nay; am I guilty of anything that is derogatory to the duties of a wife?" Likewise, Amy Hammond declared that her husband Titus had advertised her "as having departed his bed and board, which is FALSE. . . . I have, ever since my intermarriage with said Titus, lived in all the duties of the marriage covenant." Women such as Meigs and Hammond not only denied that they had deserted; they also claimed to be dutiful wives. These women knew that their right to their husbands' support depended on the faithful performance of their marital duties. Such wives understood that they could continue to charge items to their husbands' accounts only if they were able to convince shop owners and tradesmen that their behavior had been impeccable and that their husbands' accusations were unfounded.[7]

Women also knew that the common law recognized wives' right to leave husbands who did not economically support them. The law allowed these women continued access to their husbands' credit:

The husband is bound by his wife's contracts for necessaries for herself, when he refuses to provide them. . . . If he should turn her out of doors, and forbid all mankind from supplying her with necessaries, yet he would be bound to fulfill her contracts for necessaries. The case is the same if she depart from her husband with reasonable cause, and refuse to cohabit with him.

More than half of Connecticut and Vermont wives who wrote notices shared Anna Crosby's complaint that her husband "refuses to provide for me." These wives justified their desertions by pointing out their legal right to their husbands' support. They agreed with Sarah Church, who wrote, "those that do not provide for their own household, are worse than an infidel and break the marriage covenant." These women insisted that their husbands had acted improperly and that they still were entitled to all the legal rights of faithful wives.[8]

On August 18, 1798, in response to her husband William's advertisement, Anna Blanchard placed a notice in the Putney *Argus*. Blanchard denied having eloped and accused her husband of neglecting her when she was sick, "leaving me no attendance, no provision, no firewood." She claimed that she had almost died because of this treatment and closed her notice with an appeal: "And now candid reader, you may judge who is most to blame." Like Blanchard, wives who placed their own advertisements did so to contest their husbands' interpretations of the marriage contract. When couples such as the Blanchards presented their different versions of their difficulties to the public, they both drew on common law traditions governing the marriage relationship. Husbands claimed the right to command their wives' obedience and to control their wives' spending, while wives defended their right to adequate economic support. The common law supported the rights of both husbands and wives, but it offered little guidance when these rights conflicted with one another. When did a husband's legitimate right to prevent his wife from purchasing luxuries become an illegitimate attempt to deny her the necessaries of life? Where was the line that divided necessaries from luxuries? Was calico cloth a luxury or a necessity? By publicly airing their grievances, husbands and wives placed questions such as these before the courts and their communities.[9]

Commentators on the common law attempted to resolve these ambiguities, but their advice was often vague. James Kent explained that when a wife charged items to her husband's account, "If the wife goes beyond what is reasonable and prudent, the tradesman trusts the wife at his peril." The Connecticut jurist Tapping Reeve added that a husband had to pay any debt his wife contracted

> when it is such a one as wives, according to the usage of the country, commonly make. If a wife should purchase at a merchant's store such articles as wives in her rank in life usually purchase, the husband ought to be bound; for it is a fair presumption that she was authorized to do so by her husband. If however, she were to purchase a ship or yoke of oxen,

no such presumption would arise, for wives do not usually purchase ships or oxen.

Determining which purchases were "reasonable and prudent" depended on local custom and the economic status of the couple in question. The wife of a wealthy man might charge fine linens, silver table settings, and expensive wines to her husband's accounts on a regular basis; however, a poorer man's spouse would not find merchants as willing to extend her credit for similar purchases. Yet each spouse, as well as merchants, artisans, and other community members, could perceive a couple's status differently. What wives believed were necessary purchases husbands often labeled unreasonable and unjustifiable. When Samuel Cesar claimed that his wife Phebe had "contracted large debts on my account," she replied that "in one case of necessity only I took up a trifling sum on his account, and never to the value of a dollars [sic] in any other." The Cesar's marriage did not disintegrate because Phebe had charged a ship or yoke of oxen to Samuel's account. Like many New England couples, Samuel and Phebe Cesar had difficulty agreeing on what constituted an unreasonably large debt or a necessary expense, a disagreement that commentators' advice could not begin to resolve.[10]

Husbands' and wives' conflicts over spending occurred against a backdrop of economic change that made issues such as debt and women's consumer activities especially troublesome. In the late eighteenth and early nineteenth centuries, New Englanders increasingly involved themselves in a web of expanding capitalist relations. Production for the market gradually replaced the subsistence orientation that had characterized rural New England households for much of the colonial era, while a growing array of consumer goods appeared in New England homes. The adoption of genteel ideals, as well as manufacturing innovations that made possible the production of large numbers of inexpensive consumer goods, helped fuel a "consumer revolution" throughout the New England countryside.[11]

Numerous historians have analyzed the implications of these ongoing transformations for men's and women's economic activities. They point out that growing involvement in the market gradually reduced the amount and importance of women's productive labors while increasing families' dependence on earning cash to purchase necessary goods. As a result of these changes, nineteenth-century Americans drew increasingly sharp distinctions between the work place and the home, and between wage work and housework. Women's economic activities—and the meanings attached to those activities—were in flux during the early national period. Scholars analyzing these transitions note that while women still engaged in productive labor, consumer spending began to assume increased importance for women as households shifted strategies in response to economic changes.[12] The expansion of the market economy and the consumer revolution occurred unevenly, of course. Farmers in rural Vermont continued to produce goods for their own use long after residents of urban, commercial centers such as Hartford had turned to the market to meet their consumer needs. However, even in rural Vermont, merchants' newspaper advertisements reveal increasing opportunities for consumption. Merchants routinely advertised china and glass ware, silver tea sets and candlesticks, necklaces, earrings, watches, books, and shoes, as well as sugar, tea, wines, rum, flour, and other groceries.[13]

Along with increased involvement in the market and these new consumer opportunities, however, came an increased risk of debt and economic failure. Between 1790 and 1830, the American economy was quite volatile. The 1790s were years of prosperity and growth; however, in the 1810s economic hardship prevailed, thanks in part to war with Great Britain and the panic of 1819. In the 1820s, prosperity returned. Amid this cycle of boom and bust, failure constantly threatened to overshadow the potential for economic success.[14] In April of 1793, David Shaw, a wheelwright from East Windsor, Connecticut, posted an advertisement in the *Connecticut Courant* notifying his creditors that "he intends to petition the General Assembly . . . that his person and property may be exempted for the term of six years from arrest and imprisonment on account of any debt heretofore contracted." In his petition, Shaw claimed that although his "Labours[,] Industry, and good Management" had brought him prosperity earlier in life, he had "fallen into Debt, and so that, at present, he cannot extricate himself." The assembly granted Shaw's petition, allowing him a six-year reprieve from debt prosecutions. However, by 1804, Shaw was in court once more, facing prosecution for unpaid debts. In her 1812 newspaper posting, Daikis Shaw claimed that her husband had provided "no other means of support for myself and family except one peck of Bran and one dozen of Potatoes." Like many other small producers, David Shaw failed to prosper in New England's changing economy. His difficulties spilled over into his marriage, which disintegrated under the pressure of economic failure.[15]

Bankruptcy petitions such as David Shaw's appeared regularly in Connecticut and Vermont newspapers, reminding New England men of the dangers of debt. In addition, an abundance of advice literature existed to warn New Englanders of debt's perils. Newspaper essays on marriage advised husbands-to-be that "when a man has entered into the matrimonial state, it then becomes his particular duty to lessen his superfluities and to regulate his expenses in such a manner that he may live within the bounds of his income." Authors warned husbands to avoid "every unnecessary indulgence . . . in dress, drinking, or dissipation." These authors directed their statements towards husbands; however, they also recognized wives' role in reducing expenses and avoiding debt. The author of *Advice in Order to Avoid Poverty* linked husbands' work and spending habits, as well as wives' consumer activities, to men's standing with their creditors:

> The most trifling actions that effect [sic] a man's credit, are to be regarded. The sound of your hammer, at five in the morning or nine at night, heard by a creditor, makes him easy six months longer. But if he sees you at a billiard table, or hears your voice in a tavern, when you should be at work, he sends for his money the next day. Finer clothes than his wife wears, or greater expence in any particular than he affords himself, shocks his pride, and he duns you to humble you.

Like another writer, who maintained "that a man must ask his wife, whether he shall be rich or not," advice authors assumed that through their consumer activities, wives greatly influenced their husbands' economic prosperity.[16]

Assumptions regarding wives' spending habits were grounded in women's increasing responsibility for purchasing items for household consumption, a development many authors believed could be fatal to families' economic well-being. One essayist claimed that many men avoided matrimony because they feared their wives would "squander away the hard-earned profits of industry." Writers especially feared the disappearance of "those beautiful domestic creatures our country formerly abounded with, whose home was their delight, who made their own and their children's clothes, who attended to the domestic affairs of the house by assisting in all its concerns." They dreaded the rise of women who devoted themselves to harassing "their husbands and fathers for . . . money to support them in their extravagance." These authors believed that women were neglecting domestic production in favor of fashionable consumption, and in the process were impoverishing their husbands and fathers.[17]

Authors and husbands also were concerned that women's consumer spending had the potential to undermine male authority within the family. In their role as consumers, wives exercised a great deal of decision-making authority. They had to choose and inspect items, determine their quality, perhaps haggle over prices, and ultimately they had to decide whether or not to purchase. As consumers, wives acted with a certain independence, since it was not practical for them to obtain their husbands' express approval for every purchase. This consumer independence could prove problematic when husbands did not approve of their wives' purchases. Newspaper postings repeatedly demonstrate husbands' concern with debt and their wives' spending habits. Edward Barney denied his wife credit because, as he claimed, she "has wasted my property, and threatens . . . to run me into debt." Barney further explained that "I have provided a comfortable subsistence for her." Barney did not accuse his wife of deserting, but he judged her spending habits to be extravagant and denied her access to his credit.[18]

Although elopement notices confirm that couples often struggled to find a mutually acceptable level of household consumption, as a rule, husbands did not specify the amount of debt or the items that their wives purchased in their advertisements. Only one couple publicly argued over a specific item the wife purchased. Jacob Ames, Jr., accused his wife Chloe of running him into debt to the amount of thirty-five pounds. In her response, Chloe sarcastically accused her husband of overreacting and asked, "can that be a greater note of wonder, than to see a half moon brought within the narrow compass of one pair of small clothes?" Chloe Ames did not believe that paying thirty-five pounds for clothes was excessive, but her husband disagreed. Publicly denying Chloe access to his credit allowed Jacob to reassert his authority over her spending habits, an authority Chloe did not hesitate to challenge once more in her response.[19]

For his hotly contested divorce case, Elias Hall obtained a number of depositions detailing the conduct of his wife Almena. Two of the depositions exposed the link between a wife's consumer activity and her husband's authority. One woman deposed that Almena Hall "told me that she got a high priced silk gown for her daughter Rosetta, and that Mr. Hall was never the wiser for it." Another neighbor referred to the same incident in her deposition: "I also knew her to go to Mr. Hough's store and get a silk gown, without Mr. Hall's knowledge or consent, when at the same time Mr. Hough had an execution against him for about $70, and when he was very much crowded for money." Almena Hall's excessive consumption was intertwined with her lack of submission. Her refusal to allow her husband's financial difficulties to limit her purchases and her attempt to deceive him threatened her husband's economic position and his authority. By offering wives a wider array of goods, the consumer revolution threatened to turn the balance of power within marriages on its head. Instead of commanding their wives' labor and service, husbands were faced with the prospect of seeing their own labor serve their wives' consumer tastes. The many desertion notices that claimed that a wife either was "determined to run me in debt and destroy my property," was "disposed to squander away my estate," or had "threatened in a very shrewd manner, to injure my interest" confirm that many husbands believed their wives' consumer activities threatened their livelihoods and their ability to govern their households. To prevent losing control of their economic status and their wives' behavior, such husbands refused to pay their wives' debts.[20]

Court records offer further evidence of the tensions between married women's consumer activities, their right to economic support, and their legal disabilities. In 1814, a justice of the peace court heard a case brought by Justin and Elias Lyman, merchants in Hartford, Vermont, against Uriah Hayes. Rachel Hayes had charged fifty dollars' worth of goods to Uriah's account at the Lymans' store on September 16, 1813, after she had deserted. The records suggest that Uriah mounted a two-pronged defense against the Lymans' charges. He refused to pay the debt on the grounds that Rachel had charged items to his account after she had deserted and after he had written a notice denying her credit. However, although Uriah's notice was dated September 3, 1813, it did not appear in the *Vermont Republican* until the eleventh of October, after Rachel had made her purchases at the Lymans' store. Uriah also argued that the items Rachel had purchased were not necessities, but were luxuries, items the law did not require husbands to provide for their wives.[21]

Because Rachel Hayes had made her purchases before Uriah's notice appeared in the newspaper, the court attempted to discover how widespread knowledge of the Hayes's separation had been. The problem was common, for a desertion notice rarely appeared in print the same day that the wife eloped. Several days or weeks almost always elapsed between the date a husband wrote his notice and the day the notice was published. In the intervening period, husbands had to rely on oral communication of the separation to prevent merchants from allowing their wives to charge items to their accounts. The only deposition contained in the Hayes case records demonstrates that knowledge of a couple's separation might not reach all interested parties in a timely fashion. Hannah Brownell deposed "that Joel Marsh[,] Lucy Marsh[,] Mary Lovel[,] & myself was sumoned [sic] and it was talked over amongst us and stated that none of us knew nothing about the Difficulty between Uriah Hayes and his wife." The late date of his advertisement's publication and the lack of general knowledge of the couple's difficulties complicated Uriah Hayes's case.[22]

Hannah Brownell's deposition indirectly dealt with another complicating factor: the couple's reconciliation. Because of the reconciliation, determining the type of goods that Rachel had purchased and discovering what had become of them were important questions for the court to answer. According to the common law, if a couple reconciled, the husband became liable for debts his wife contracted to obtain necessaries during the separation. The Lymans insisted that Rachel had purchased necessaries that she had used to support herself during the couple's estrangement. The list of goods Rachel charged at the Lymans' store included plates, bowls, cups and saucers, knives, forks, and teaspoons, various tools for sewing, and a variety of cloth, including muslin, calico, silk, satin, and lace. She also ordered chocolate, sugar, and tea. While many of these items might not have qualified as necessaries, they apparently did not exceed what the Lymans believed was appropriate for a woman of Rachel Hayes's social position. The court had to determine whether all of these items were necessaries that Rachel used to support herself during the separation or luxuries that her husband had the right to deny her. In her deposition Brownell stated, "Mrs. Lovel said she knows nothing of the difficulty [between Rachel and Uriah] only she knew about the goods what became of part of them." Unfortunately, the deposition does not record what Lovel knew about the goods Rachel had obtained.[23]

The court decided that all of the goods qualified as necessaries that Rachel had used to support herself during the separation and ordered Uriah Hayes to pay the Lymans fifty-two dollars. Hayes appealed to the Windsor County Civil Court. However, the records do not reveal that court's disposition of the case. The justice of the peace court had supported a wife's right to her husband's support. By accepting a broad definition of what purchases constituted necessaries, the court also supported wives' right to demand support at a level appropriate to the couple's economic status. Uriah Hayes was very well off: when the couple divorced in 1819, court records reveal that his estate was worth over four thousand dollars. The local court determined that luxuries such as table settings and fine cloth were appropriate items for the wife of a wealthy man to obtain at her husband's expense. Although neither Rachel nor Uriah Hayes may have welcomed this decision, the court had demonstrated it could not easily dismiss wives' right to their husbands' economic support.[24]

In spite of its support for wives' rights, the court's decision in the Hayes case did not threaten husbands' authority over their wives. Uriah Hayes failed in his attempt to use his legal power to deny his wife access to his credit. However, he only failed because his wife returned to his household. The court supported Rachel Hayes's right to economic support during the couple's separation because she ultimately had submitted to her husband's authority. Only when wives assumed their place as dependent subordinates would the courts grant them the right to their husbands' support. By defending wives' rights to economic support as long as the women acknowledged their husbands' authority over them, the court protected the traditional hierarchical marriage contract.

Wives' right to economic support intertwined with their economic dependence on their husbands. When the courts demanded that husbands support their wives, they did so because they refused to acknowledge that married women could act as independent economic agents. Although wives who charged goods to their husbands' accounts without obtaining their spouses' express permission to do so appeared to be acting independently, legal commentators insisted that "the presumption is that the husband assents to all the engagements of the wife which are necessary and proper in the domestic economy of the family." Presuming the husband's assent to his wife's purchases rendered legally invisible any independent judgment or act that the wife might make while purchasing. The law made no provision for a husband who could not control his wife's spending habits. When discussing husbands' obligation to pay for necessities their wives charged to their accounts, Zephaniah Swift addressed and dismissed the possibility that a wife could defy her husbands' wishes successfully: "Nor is it any excuse that the wife is unmanageable and disobedient, as he ought to exercise his marital rights and regulate her conduct." Husbands who posted notices denying their wives credit were attempting to exercise their marital rights; however, the notices themselves, along with wives' responses, indicate that negotiating an acceptable level of consumer spending was far more complicated than Swift and other commentators acknowledged.[25]

While obscuring the very real conflicts between spouses over the issue of consumer spending, legal commentators' and courts' refusal to acknowledge wives' independent economic action could either harm or help particular men's economic interests while strengthening *all* husbands' authority over their wives. An 1826 Vermont Supreme Court case, *Franklin Robinson v. Elisha Reynolds, & Sally, his wife,* demonstrates the emphasis courts placed on maintaining husbands' authority regardless of the actual financial effects of the courts' decisions on the husbands and merchants involved. In October of 1816, Franklin Robinson had delivered merchandise to Sally, who then was married to Joseph Emmerson. Robinson claimed that Joseph Emmerson had deserted Sally in 1812 and that she lived in South Hero "separate and apart from the said Joseph, and was there trading and doing business as a single woman, and sole trader . . . the said Franklin did not give any credit to the said Joseph, but traded and dealt with the said Sally, as a *feme sole,* and on her sole credit." Robinson's attorney argued that because the state divorce statute allowed divorce on the grounds of three years' willful desertion, "the husband loses all power to reclaim the wife against her consent, by a *wilful desertion* for more than three years; and that, consequently, she is then free to contract, and bound by her contracts." Robinson believed that because he had delivered merchandise to Sally more than four years after her first husband's desertion, Sally was operating legally as a single woman. Therefore, she and her current husband were liable for the debt she had incurred. The Reynoldses argued that at the time Robinson delivered the merchandise, Sally was a *feme covert* and therefore not liable for any contracts she made. They believed that Joseph Emmerson, Sally's legal husband at the time of the transaction, was liable for the debt.[26]

The court found for the Reynoldses on the grounds that "there is no principle of law, that will authorize her [a married woman] to sue, or subject her to a suit, as a *feme sole* . . . on account of his [the husband's] temporary absence." The court decreed that a married woman legally could not act as an independent economic agent, even if she had been living apart from her husband for many years. In the eyes of the law, deserted wives remained economically dependent on their husbands. The court affirmed the fact that married women had no independent legal existence apart from their husbands. This lack of independence dictated the court's insistence that husbands support their wives and pay any debts the women contracted. According to the law, married women's most important right stemmed from their legal and economic dependence. Of course, the support that wives could expect from their husbands came at a price: if a husband who deserted his wife remained legally responsible for her debts, he also was able to return and exercise full authority over her. As the Vermont justices explained, "The Court cannot listen to the suggestion, that the husband, by three years absence, has lost all right to reclaim the wife without her consent; nor will absence alone, for any length of time, deprive the husband of his legal rights, as such, over the wife." As in the Hayes case, the court supported a wife's right to economic support only when the husband could exercise his authority over her. Had Joseph Emmerson returned, he legally could have cohabited with Sally and received any property she had accumulated in his absence even if she had not wanted a reconciliation. The possibility that Emmerson could return and resume his position of authority within his marriage guaranteed both his wife's right to his support and her continuing dependent status.[27]

If Franklin Robinson wanted payment for the goods he delivered to Sally, he would have to sue Joseph Emmerson. Because Emmerson never had returned, it is reasonable to assume that Robinson could not recover payment. From the court's perspective, upholding husbands' authority over their wives was far more important than protecting the economic interests of one merchant. And while Sally and Elisha Reynolds no doubt welcomed this outcome, the court's decision may have made merchants across the state less willing to extend credit to any married woman living apart from her husband. A decision that upheld wives' right to economic support from their husbands may have limited estranged wives' ability to support themselves. Without any means of support, such women may have been forced to come to terms with their husbands and to submit to the men's authority, a state of affairs that would have pleased the court.

Both the limitations and opportunities that existed for married women in early national New England stemmed from wives' legal and economic disabilities. When they married, women lost the right to own their own property, wages, and labor. Legally, wives were dependent subordinates, incapable of independent action in the economic arena. Women's subordinate position within the marriage relationship placed them under their husbands' authority. Husbands held legal power over their wives' living arrangements and consumer behavior. Men could compel their wives' obedience by withdrawing the women's access to their credit. Yet, these legal disabilities entitled wives to their husbands' economic support. In addition, new opportunities for wives to make independent consumer decisions held the potential to moderate wives' subordination even as they created additional possibilities for marital conflict. Women themselves were active agents in asserting their own interests. Wives purchased items without their husbands' knowledge or consent, and they forcefully defended their right to adequate economic support. However, wives understood the extent to which their rights intertwined with their disabilities, and they were careful to present themselves as faithful wives who had fulfilled their marital obligations. When petitioning for divorce from her husband, James, on the grounds of adultery and desertion, Fanny Gladding complained that she had been "disappointed in her expectations of conjugal comfort and support." However, Gladding knew that she deserved comfort and support only because she had lived with her husband "in the due performance of all the duties of the marriage covenant."[28] Once again, married women could claim their rights only if they behaved in ways that affirmed their status as the weaker, dependent spouse. Wives attempted to balance the submission and dependence that the marriage contract required of them with their individual interests and desires. Their struggle to do so illuminates the contradictions inherent in matrimony's unequal bargain.

3

"The Duties of a Wife"
The Meaning of Women's Work

On March 23, 1795, Asa Goodenow printed a notice in the *Rutland Herald*: "Whereas Hannah, my Wife, refuses to labour, and says she will run me into Debt, this is to forbid all Persons trusting her on my account, for I will not pay any debt of her contracting after this date."[1] Goodenow was concerned that his wife's consumer behavior might run him into debt; however, he also was dissatisfied because Hannah would not perform the labors that the traditional marriage contract assigned to women. Although new consumer opportunities created tensions within marriages in the early republic, notices such as Goodenow's reveal that couples also struggled with the traditional economic obligations of matrimony. Husbands and wives shared a belief in the centrality of economic responsibilities to the marriage contract. However, men and women perceived both the economic exchange that lay at the heart of the marriage relationship and the balance of power within that relationship in very different ways. Men perceived their marriages according to hierarchical norms, which stressed women's subordination to and dependence on their husbands, whereas wives' experiences led them to believe that they and their husbands were interdependent partners. Desertion postings reveal that couples struggled to reconcile the legal fact of wives' economic dependence on their husbands with the reality of marriage as an economic partnership.

New Englanders' increasing involvement in the market as both producers and consumers complicated couples' attempts to negotiate the meaning of women's work. Although wives' consumer activities increased throughout the early nineteenth century, women continued to engage in a great deal of productive labor, both for their families' use and for the market. Jeanne Boydston has demonstrated that in spite of the tremendous amount of work that women performed, Americans increasingly devalued women's household labors in the early national period. House-holds' greater involvement in the market placed a heightened importance on wage-earning activities; because most housework did not earn cash, it lost recognition as real work. Instead, Americans in the early republic began to perceive the performance of household work as a natural ex-pression of women's domestic nature. This "pastoralization of house-work" became the dominant view of women's domestic labors in the nineteenth century and beyond.[2]

This ideological transition regarding what constituted real work pre-cipitated a contest between husbands and wives, one that elopement no-tices and divorce petitions provide an opportunity to examine. These sources reveal that New England women struggled against their hus-bands' attempts to render their labors invisible. Married women believed their work was vitally important to their families' economic survival. Rather than seeing themselves as economically dependent on their hus-bands, unable to act in their own interests or on their own initiative, mar-ried women believed that they were partners with their husbands in sup-porting their families. This belief sometimes led wives to take actions that exceeded the legal boundaries governing married women's economic ac-tivities. Wives even articulated a view of property ownership within mar-riage that, because of their economic contributions, recognized married women's claim to certain types of property. Husbands recognized the im-portance of women's work; however, they claimed ownership of their wives' labors and presented themselves as the primary source of their families' economic support. These couples' words and experiences illu-minate a crucial contest over who would control and claim ownership of women's labor, revealing that marriages were not immune to the conflicts over the division of labor and allocation of resources that characterized the economic landscape in the transition to market capitalism.[3]

The labor of both husbands and wives was essential to family survival in New England, although the types of work men and women performed differed according to whether they lived in more rural or urban settings and according to each household's relative involvement in the market. Vermont remained overwhelmingly rural, and most Vermonters contin-ued to work in agriculture throughout the early nineteenth century. Early nineteenth-century Connecticut's economy was much more reliant on commercial and manufacturing activities than was Vermont's; however, according to the 1820 census, the majority of Hartford County residents continued to labor in agriculture.[4] Although Connecticut had more urban areas than Vermont, residents of Connecticut's country towns engaged in a mix of economic activities that would have been familiar to Vermonters and other rural New Englanders.[5] Many New England farmers combined agriculture with a trade, as did Ansel Cowdery of Woodstock, Vermont, a basketmaker who also ran a small farm between 1800 and his death in 1868, or Samuel Metcalf, a saddler who farmed ninety acres in Royalton, Vermont, between 1790 and 1855. With the exception of urban areas such as Windsor, Vermont, or Hartford, Connecticut, local markets in these states were too small to enable many artisans to support themselves solely by practicing their trade. Nor was farming a sure road to prosperity in a region where frosts in late May and early September significantly shortened the growing season. Rural New Englanders responded to these unfavorable conditions by diversifying: while growing staples for their own subsistence, they also produced more marketable commodities, such as maple syrup, or the timber that David and Anna Crosby sold from their farm in Lebanon, Connecticut.[6]

Providing for a family under these circumstances required tremendous amounts of labor from both husbands and wives. In his *Natural and Political History of the State of Vermont,* published in 1798, Ira Allen briefly described the typical labors of men and women in rural New England: "The men willingly assume all the toils of the field, and every species of servile labour. Women are employed in the concerns of the house, such as preparing the frugal repast, spinning, weaving, knitting, etc."[7] On New England farms, men cleared land, raised and marketed crops, tended livestock and sheep, and built and repaired buildings, fences, and tools. Women tended dairy cattle, poultry, and vegetable gardens, prepared and preserved food, made, cleaned, and mended clothing, bore and cared for children, and made a variety of items for household use, such as butter, cheese, soap, and candles. While men's work varied with the seasons and provided them with opportunities for socializing—especially when taking produce to market—women's work tended to be monotonous and confined them to the home. A New England broadside captured the contrast between the rhythms of men's work and women's labors:

> The farmer sat in his easy-chair,
> Smoking his pipe of clay,
> While his hale old wife with busy care
> Was clearing the dishes away . . .
> The house-dog lay stretched out on the floor,

> Where the shade, after noon, used to steal,
> The busy old wife by the open door,
> Was turning the spinning wheel . . .
> Still the farmer sat in his easy-chair . . .
> His head, bent down . . . Fast asleep. . . .

Men could afford some leisure time away from work, but a series of never-ending tasks dominated rural women's days and left them little time to nap in their easy chairs.[8]

The labor of both husbands and wives was no less crucial to New England's urban dwellers. In the early national period, Hartford city had the largest population (7,074 by 1830) and the most diverse economy of any community in either Hartford, Connecticut, or Windsor, Vermont, counties. In the early nineteenth century, Hartford boasted paper and powder mills, glass works, tanneries, and cotton and woolen factories, along with numerous small producers such as cabinet makers, chair makers, and clothiers. In 1825, three banks, three insurance companies, Washington College, the American Asylum for the Deaf and Dumb, and a full complement of Missionary and Ladies' Aid Societies testified to the presence of a prosperous middle class.[9] In contrast, the economy of Windsor, Vermont (population 3,094 in 1830), was diverse, but on a smaller scale. In the early nineteenth century, Windsor was home to several printing houses, binderies, and saddleries, a tannery, a bark mill factory, a grist mill, and a woolen factory, as well as watchmakers, a coach and chaise maker, and other small producers. A number of lawyers, ministers, doctors, and merchants made up a small middle class.[10]

Windsor, Vermont, was not the commercial and manufacturing center that Hartford city was, but it shared with Hartford increasingly sharp divisions among unskilled workers, small artisans and mechanics, and the middle class. The economic strategies of each of these groups were quite distinct; however, women's labor was crucial for success in each case. Working-class women worked for wages as domestics and laundresses, while the wives of artisans and mechanics were a crucial source of labor in their small shops. Middle-class urban women engaged in a mix of household production and consumer activities. It was not uncommon for urban wives to keep cows and chickens, as well as to tend vegetable gardens in order to provide food for their families. Throughout the course of the early nineteenth century, however, consumption gradually replaced production as the dominant way that middle-class urban families met their needs.[11]

Husbands' desertion notices and divorce petitions reveal that the variety of tasks and amount of labor women performed were indispensable to family survival. The most common complaint that New England husbands voiced in their desertion postings was that their wives refused to perform their household duties and were behaving in ways the men judged to be inappropriate.[12] Many men echoed Ezra Dunham, who claimed his wife Mary had "violated the marriage covenant, by refusing to perform the duties of a Wife." When petitioning for divorce, James Gladding accused his wife Fanny of desertion; he claimed that she had lived "in the total neglect of all the duties and offices" of the marriage covenant and that she had not "afforded to your petitioner that aid and comfort which by said covenant she was bound to do." Likewise, Moses Rood lamented that his wife "refuses any longer to assist me in the support of my family," and John Roberts complained that his wife Rebecka "refuses to live with me or do any kind of work for me." What displeased these men most was their wives' refusal to perform the labors that the marriage contract assigned to women. Husbands believed that they were entitled to their wives' service, and wives' refusal, or inability, to serve them well was a major source of marital dissatisfaction for men.[13]

Although New England wives performed a variety of tasks, husbands' complaints reveal the overriding importance of two types of female labor: food preparation and the manufacture and care of clothing. Nathan Foster complained that Betsy Foster "refuses to do my necessary cooking and washing." Joseph Lovel composed a poem that detailed the duties neglected by his wife Suke:

> For she will neither spin nor weave,
> But there she'll sit and take her ease;
> There she'll sit, and pout and grin,
> As if the Devil had entered in;
> For she would neither knit nor sew,
> But all in rags I had to go:
> So, farewel Suke! and farewel, wife!
> Till you can live a better life.

In the depositions that Elias Hall collected for his divorce, his wife Almena's lack of attention to meal preparation and Elias's clothing figures prominently. One neighbor deposed that "when Mr. Hall was at work on his farm . . . and came home for his meals, his wife would have nothing prepared for him to eat, and if he spoke to her on the subject, she replied with a frown, 'If you want to eat you must get your own victuals.'" Another neighbor claimed that Mrs. Hall "said she would not wash a shirt for Mr. Hall if she knew it would be the means of saving his life. . . . Mrs. Hall wholly refused to mend or make for Mr. Hall, and I found his clothes in a very bad condition." These husbands' complaints reveal the fundamental importance of women's productive activities. Wives' refusal to attend to their household duties was not mere inconvenience; it threatened real hardship and deprivation to entire families.[14]

Women's productive work was necessary for family subsistence; yet elopement notices also offer evidence that wives assisted their husbands in more commercial endeavors. When Curtis Hale advertised his wife's desertion, he added, "I do also forbid any payment to her of any debt now due, or that shall hereafter become due to me." Hale's debtors had been accustomed to settling their accounts with Sally Hale; her desertion threatened the continued success of her husband's business. Likewise, Edward Wood complained that his wife, Submitte, was "unable to trade or transact business of much importance to advantage, or to my satisfaction." The custom of allowing a wife to act as her husband's agent facilitated men's commercial transactions; however, in the event of marital conflict, wives could inflict financial harm on their husbands. Men like Jason Perkins, who maintained that his wife was "unfit to buy and sell and make bargains," and Samuel Jones, who complained that his wife Rachel "has for a long time past, traded and disposed of my property unknown to me," revealed the centrality of their wives' economic responsibilities to family survival *and* to marital conflict.[15]

When Robert Bloomer complained that his wife Betsey "has denied doing her duty," the specific tasks that he believed his wife had neglected might have included preparing meals, mending clothes, or acting as his agent. Regardless of what specific tasks these wives had not performed, their husbands believed that the women had acted in a manner that was damaging to their interests. The common law and social custom equated the family's interest with the interest of the household head, the husband. Chancellor James Kent stated that "the husband is the best judge of the wants of the family, and the means of supplying them." Law and custom expected wives to comply with what their husbands judged to be in their families' interests. After he accused Betsey of not performing her duties, Robert Bloomer elaborated that she had neglected "attending to the concerns of her family." Husbands such as Bloomer believed that their wives should labor on behalf of their families, and they claimed the right to determine what activities were and were not in their families' interests.[16]

New England wives shared their husbands' concern with the economic responsibilities of the marriage contract. Their husbands' failure to provide adequate economic support was the most common complaint that appeared in women's desertion postings and divorce petitions.[17] Rachel Martin claimed that her husband John had "wilfully refused and neglected to provide in any degree for the support of myself and family." Like many other women petitioning for divorce, Lucretia Hill accused her husband of having "wholly neglected to furnish the petitioner with any support." Tabitha Austens wanted to leave no doubt in the minds of her advertisement's readers about her husband's failure to support her when she wrote, "What he provided for me for one year is as follows:—One pound of rusty pork, one peck of meal, one half peck of beans, one half bushel of potatoes, and four ounces of wool." These women believed their spouses had violated the most basic right the marriage contract guaranteed to wives: their husbands' economic support.[18]

When they married, these women gave up their legal identities, their wages, and any property they owned in exchange for their husbands' support. Much of their marital discontent stemmed from the fact that their husbands could not or would not provide that support. Elizabeth Hamblin lamented that her husband "has not provided anything for the sustenance of myself or our children, but has ordered me to go off and get my living where I can." But she continued, "Notwithstanding Simeon Hamblin has thus ordered me and forced me to leave him, still I am willing to live with him, if he will provide for his family a habitation." Elizabeth Hamblin understood the importance of both husbands' and wives' labor to family survival. Her willingness to return to live with a man who had forced her to leave, if he would live up to his basic economic obligations, reveals the continuing importance of economic exchange in marriages of the early republic.[19]

In spite of husbands' and wives' shared concern for the economic obligations of the marriage contract, tensions existed between their different interpretations of how the performance or neglect of these obligations affected the balance of power within their relationships. Men held a legalistic, hierarchical view of marriage's economic relationship. Presenting themselves as the primary source of their families' (and wives') support, husbands obscured the real significance of their spouses' labor. By granting husbands ownership of the products of women's labor and identifying married women as economic dependents, the law also helped render invisible wives' work and stressed women's reliance on men's economic activities. Married women articulated a very different view of their position within the household and in relation to their husbands. Women claimed ownership of their own labors and believed that their economic contributions entitled them to a claim of partnership with their husbands. Wives recognized their dependence on their husbands, but they also claimed that their husbands were equally dependent on women's labor. Husbands' insistence on wives' economic subordination and wives' desire for a more egalitarian partnership provided the backdrop against which couples aired their marital discontent and attempted to resolve their differences.

The very act of printing notices to deny their wives credit indicates that these husbands thought of their spouses as economic dependents. Legally, of course, the husbands were correct: married women could not own their own property or lay claim to their own wages. Married women could not contract debts in their own names, but had to rely on their husbands' credit. Husbands believed that their spouses' legal and economic dependence gave them the right to control their wives' behavior. By removing his economic support and by insisting on his wife's good behavior and the dutiful performance of her housework, a husband was acting on his legal rights as the economic head of the family. However, in their descriptions of their marriage relationships, women challenged the economic authority of their husbands and claimed identities at odds with their husbands' insistence on subordination and dependence. In her response to her husband Thomas's advertisement, Hannah West accused him of deserting and claimed that he "has taken from me all my cloth that I had to clothe my family with, & all my yarn that I had spinned . . . in my absence he carried away my flax, wool, and all the provisions which we raised on our farm the last year, which was enough to have supported our family, and to have sold to the amount of 200 dollars, had it been taken care of in a prudent manner." West's posting described some of her work roles and proclaimed West's view of herself as an economic producer and provider. West presented herself as her husband's partner; indeed, her assertions of property ownership, her valuation of the provisions she and Thomas had raised, and her implicit claim that she could have managed affairs more prudently than her husband demonstrate that West's intimate involvement in the family's economic affairs was a central component of her identity. The law recognized Thomas West as the economic head of household, but Hannah West held a very strong belief in the importance of her contributions to the household economy and she believed that she, and not her husband, was the best judge of what was in her family's interests.[20]

Other women also maintained that their labor had been of equal or even greater importance than their husbands' in supporting their families. Lucy Martin declared that her husband had "ever since our unfortunate marriage, lived by the Fruit of my industry principally." Sarah Hall warned her husband's creditors not to "call on me for his debts, as I have maintained the gentleman for two years, and instead of my elopement he has run away himself—and I offer no reward for his return." Clarissa Post claimed that she had supported her husband for a long time but was "determined to do it no longer," and Sarah Church assured those in her community that she would not try to charge items to her husband's accounts, while warning that "neither will I pay any more of his debts, as I have done heretofore." These wives' experiences led them to believe that they were producers and providers in their own right, and that they were entitled to the recognition, respect, and control over resources that were commensurate with those identities.[21]

The forcefulness with which these women presented their versions of their marital disputes belies stereotypes of early American women as docile subordinates, trapped in a psychology of dependence that social custom and common law traditions of coverture reinforced. The legal disabilities inherent in married women's status as *femes covert* and the patriarchal nature of marriage as a legal and economic institution did not create truly dependent women. Wives' desertion notices reveal a counterweight to the numerous legal, psychological, and ideological impediments to married women's ability to act in their own interests. The experiences that women such as Hannah West and Lucy Martin described in their postings ran counter to their legal status as dependent subordinates. These women's experiences led them to recognize that their labor was essential to their families' well-being. Therefore, they did not view themselves as economic dependents of their husbands. In spite of the law's insistence that the man was the economic head of his family, these women knew that the labor of both husbands and wives was necessary for economic survival. New England wives insisted that their contributions to the household economy were essential, and they insisted that they were entitled to receive concrete benefits in exchange for their labors. In 1813, Esther Green printed a notice in which she claimed that her husband had required that she sign an agreement to "relinquish all claim on him and his property" before he turned over to her the property she had brought into the marriage. Green had been ill and her husband had wanted her to use her own property, not his, to pay her expenses during her illness. Green left her husband, not only because of his miserly actions while she was ill but also because "he has ever since refused to come to any agreement or to allow me in any way any benefit for my work when my health should be restored." Like many other New England wives, Esther Green recognized that her labor was valuable and she believed that she deserved a share of the benefits her work would bring to her household.[22]

These wives recognized the importance of their domestic labors because of the nature of New England's economy. Although much of women's housework did not earn cash, many products of rural women's labors provided vital links to local networks of neighborly exchange and to the broader market economy. In 1826, in response to her husband's posting, Mary Prentice denied having deserted and claimed that "I never left your house only to set up my loom at your son Edgcoms to weave for you to pay a debt." Prentice's weaving to repay a debt was typical of the transactions that characterized rural neighborly exchange. The cloth that Prentice wove, and the butter, cheese, and eggs that were the products of women's labors, did earn "cash"—or, more accurately, credit—that enabled families to pay their debts and to purchase items that they could not produce. When women such as Phebe Darling responded to their husbands' advertisements by stating, "I . . . shall henceforth pay no debts of his contracting on any account whatever, as heretofore I have done," they were referring to the practice of using women's labor to settle accounts with neighbors and merchants.[23]

In the early national period, husbands who wrote elopement notices were quick to point out wives' increased consumer activities while obscuring the importance of women's production for the market. However, the expanding market economy provided women with opportunities for both increased consumption and increased production. One historian's analysis of women's purchases at a Worcester, Massachusetts, store in 1809 and 1817 reveals that women most frequently purchased items required for the manufacture of clothing and other household linens. Cloth, sewing tools and equipment, yarn, trimmings and buttons, as well as knitting, spinning, and weaving equipment made up the bulk of these women's purchases.[24] Women, in other words, most commonly purchased items to use in their household labors. Their consumer activities were inextricably linked with household production.

In 1809, Aaron and John Buckland, merchants in East Hartford, Connecticut, sued Daniel Hill for unpaid debts. The Bucklands submitted a list of the items charged against and credited to Hill's account in 1806. Someone had charged a shawl, several different kinds of cloth, buttons, and a vest pattern against Hill's account. The Bucklands also had credited ninety-one cents to Hill's account, the value of thirteen pounds of butter they had received on his behalf. The Bucklands' account does not indicate who made these purchases or who brought the butter to their store. Clearly, however, women's labors underlay both the purchases and the credit. The majority of items purchased—the cloth, buttons, and pattern —were raw materials that women's labor would transform into clothing. Likewise, women's labor had produced the butter that provided Daniel Hill with some credit. Years earlier, Hill had posted a notice declaring that he would no longer pay his wife Clarissa's debts. The notice did not contain an accusation of desertion; it only indicated that Hill was displeased with the amount of debt his wife had contracted. On its own, the notice highlights Clarissa Hill's consumer behavior and suggests that she was responsible for the purchases later made at the Bucklands' store. The Bucklands' account, however, complicates the picture of Clarissa Hill as a spendthrift wife. Clarissa Hill's consumer activities provided materials she needed for her labors, and her labors helped finance her purchases. The market economy offered women an opportunity to challenge their husbands' authority by purchasing items without their spouses' permission *and* an avenue to improve their families' welfare by producing such items as butter and cheese, which they could exchange for family necessities. Elopement notices such as Daniel Hill's obscured women's labors by focusing on their consumer spending. Without acknowledging the degree to which women's work and women's purchases were intertwined, such notices rendered invisible the significance of wives' household labors.[25]

The issue of property ownership within marriage best illustrates the different meanings that husbands and wives assigned to women's labors, as well as the difficulties that husbands and wives faced as they attempted to reconcile legal realities, changing ideologies of work, and lived experience. Women's conviction that their economic contributions were vitally important led them to claim ownership of certain household items, regardless of the law's insistence that their husbands owned this property. Like Hannah West, who accused her husband of stealing *her* cloth, yarn, flax, and wool, other women asserted proprietary rights over particular objects. Dolly Dodge accused her husband of selling "all my household furniture" and Thankful Hutchens claimed that her husband had driven her away and prevented her from taking "any of my cloathing [sic], money, or other property." The objects women most frequently claimed to own were personal items, such as Thankfull Hutchens's clothing (to which the common law recognized wives' legal claim), household furnishings and utensils, especially those they had brought into the marriage, and the products of their own labors, such as cloth or produce from gardens or dairies. In other words, women believed that their property rights extended to the things they produced or used in their household labors. Women also recognized their husbands' proprietary claim to those objects with which men worked. After accusing her husband of stealing *her* property, Hannah West went on to speak of *"his* farm, horses, cows, hogs, etc." These wives recognized a division of property rights that mirrored the gendered division of labor in New England households.[26]

Women who wrote newspaper notices based their property claims on their contributions to the household economy. They believed that they and their husbands were partners in the family enterprise and that they were entitled to claim ownership of certain property because of their status as partners. New England women hoped for mutuality within the marriage relationship on the basis of the work they performed with their husbands to support their families. In her study of farm women in nineteenth-century New York, Nancy Grey Osterud argues that because rural wives contributed to production for the market in significant ways, they fostered "an ethic of mutuality in work and decision making between husbands and wives." She demonstrates that farm men and women engaged in shared tasks, such as slaughtering and processing livestock, and that men and women both engaged in subsistence and market-oriented labors. A clear gendered division of labor existed on these New York farms; however, Osterud reveals that men and women crossed this gendered divide when it was necessary. This type of household work environment helped create marriages based on mutuality and interdependence and seems consistent with the labor patterns that New England women described in their newspaper postings. In their advertisements, Connecticut and Vermont women clearly indicated their desire for mutuality and partnership with their husbands, a desire that was rooted in the shared experience of providing for their families.[27]

The New England men who wrote elopement notices, however, did not share their wives' mutualistic views on economic partnership and property ownership. Dozens of husbands accused their wives of stealing the very objects that women believed they owned. Jedidiah Dudley accused his wife of taking "much of my furniture." Peter Tatro claimed his wife had stolen "every article of furniture, cooking utensils, etc.," and Thomas Lewis informed the public that his wife had "carried off and concealed a considerable part of my household furniture and bedding." Bedding, furniture, and cooking utensils were the types of property many women brought with them into marriage and they were the objects that women, more than men, used in their household labors. Understandably, women came to regard these things as their own, but husbands did not recognize their wives' claims. Joseph Sanborn accused his wife Clarissa of stealing "all the property that I brought with her when I moved her home." Like Sanborn, even when their wives had brought property into the marriage, husbands considered themselves to be the sole owners of that property and refused to acknowledge their wives' claims to ownership, a perception that was consistent with emerging ideologies that devalued women's work and highlighted wives' dependence on their husbands for support.[28]

The law also did not recognize these wives' property claims. Regardless of how much effort a woman expended in improving her family's welfare or how much property a woman brought into marriage, unless she was protected by a special trust agreement, her labor and her property, with the exception of personal effects such as clothing and jewelry, legally belonged to her husband. A husband's legal right to his wife's wages and property left married women who had deserted or had been deserted in an especially vulnerable position. Their husbands or their husbands' creditors could disrupt these women's efforts to support themselves by asserting ownership of their wages or produce. When Mary Smith petitioned for a divorce from her husband in 1813, she accused him of deserting and claimed that "she is much embarrassed, having frequently to offset the demands of the sd [sic] Marshals creditors when attempting in his name to collect her own earnings and thereby put to great inconvenience in obtaining a scanty subsistence for herself and family." Obtaining a divorce allowed Mary Smith to collect wages in her own name, free from the claims of her husband's creditors.[29]

The common law's insistence that husbands owned all property did not prevent Connecticut and Vermont women from claiming property as their own. However, Connecticut and Vermont courts interpreted property law quite differently. The Vermont Supreme Court showed some sympathy for wives' property claims, while the Connecticut courts proved to be more conservative when hearing cases that concerned married women's property. The differences between the legal settings within which Vermont and Connecticut women lived confirm that the common law was far from a monolithic construct. Instead, the varied statutes, customs, and circumstances of each state determined the context within which the courts applied the common law. These different legal contexts helped shape the possibilities available to married women claiming property ownership.[30]

The Vermont Supreme Court provided some support for wives' property claims and economic responsibilities. At least fifty-three of the eighty-two women—65 percent—who petitioned the Vermont Supreme Court for alimony between 1790 and 1830 succeeded. These alimony awards testify to the court's (and taxpayers') concern that divorced women be provided the opportunity to support themselves and their children. Aware of this concern, Vermont wives requesting alimony often asserted their ability to contribute to their families' support. Rachel Nichols addressed the economic concerns of the court directly in her petition: "your Petitioner does not consider herself in like need of going upon the Town—that the amount of Estate and effects which she brought to her said Husband is sufficient . . . to support herself independently during the remainder of her life." Betsey Downer accused her husband of driving her from his house and claimed that she "has ever since been obliged to subsist by her own personal labor and the charity of her friends." Abigail Niles reported that since her husband's desertion she had received support "by her own industry or from the charity of friends." Most women did not claim to be able to support themselves on their own; they needed friends and other family members to fill the economic gap that their husbands' absence created. However, they presented themselves to the court as fully capable of upholding their end of matrimony's economic contract. These women believed that alimony awards would help them continue to fulfill their economic obligations.[31]

The state supreme court's alimony awards demonstrate a degree of support for the female definition of family property. In their desertion postings, women claimed to own the property they had brought into their marriages as well as the items that they produced or used in their household labors. While the marriage endured, this property legally belonged to their husbands, but upon marital dissolution the women's view of property ownership prevailed. The type of property the Vermont court most frequently awarded to women was household furniture and utensils, the objects women most frequently claimed to own in their desertion notices (See table 1). The court awarded women land less than half as frequently as household furnishings. In three-quarters of the instances in which the court did award land to the woman, she either had children to support or she had brought the real estate in question into the marriage. The court hesitated to take real estate from a lawful male owner; only the fact that it would support his heirs made the redistribution of landed property palatable.[32]

The divorce of Nancy and Benjamin Page best reveals the Vermont court's position concerning the gendered division of property. Nancy and Benjamin had married on April 25, 1793, in Hartland, Vermont. They had at least two children and lived on a farm in Hartland until May 1, 1804, when Nancy claimed that Benjamin had deserted after treating her with intolerable severity. Benjamin did not go far, for he appeared in August 1810, when the court heard Nancy's petition for a divorce and request for alimony. The court granted her both and ordered Benjamin to return to Nancy the property she had inherited from her father. The justices confirmed her title to all of her personal property and to all the household furniture and utensils. In addition, they awarded her half of all the land and buildings on the farm to support herself and the couple's children. Although she received only half of the land, the court ordered that Nancy be allowed to reap all of the crops she had sown on the entire farm that year.[33]

TABLE I

Vermont Supreme Court Alimony Awards, 1790–1830

Based on 53 Awards in Chittenden, Washington, and Windsor Counties

Type	No. of Times Awarded[a]	Percentage of Awards[b]
Furniture/Utensils	38	72
Cash	22	41
Land	16	30
Livestock	8	15

[a] Because the court often included several types of property in one award, the total number of times each property type was awarded exceeds the number of awards.

[b] The percentage of awards containing the specific property type. Again, because the court often included several property types in one award, the total percentages exceed 100 percent.

The principles guiding the Vermont court in this alimony decision are strikingly similar to those that women articulated in their elopement notices. Those women claimed ownership of the property they had brought into marriage; similarly, the court restored her father's legacy to Nancy Page. Women who wrote desertion notices claimed ownership of the things they produced or used in their household labors. Nancy Page received the household furniture and utensils, as well as the crops she had produced. Women in desertion postings presented themselves as economic partners, actively engaged in providing support for their families. The court recognized Nancy Page's ability to support her family economically and provided her with the means to continue to do so.

The similarities between the Vermont Supreme Court's alimony decisions and the views on property ownership and economic partnership that women presented in their desertion notices had their limits. The Vermont court never recognized any married woman's claim to own property separately from her husband. Only when a marriage legally ended did the court agree that women had a greater claim to certain types of property than did men. The Vermont justices did not intend for their recognition of married women's claim to property to support women's independence. The fact that the court most often awarded women household furniture and utensils suggests that the justices intended to provide women with the tools they would need to perform their traditional labors in another household, whether it be that of a second husband or that of a kinsman. In this context, the court's customary recognition of women's property rights within marriage was compatible with the law's insistence that women remain economically dependent on men.

In its alimony decisions, the Vermont Supreme Court was especially careful to restore to divorced women the property that they had brought into their marriages. In an 1802 case, Edward Gould asked the supreme court to uphold a lease agreement he had signed with William Webster, allowing him to rent some of Webster's land. However, Webster's wife had brought this particular piece of property into the marriage, and after the couple divorced, the wife insisted that the lease should be terminated because she had never agreed to it. The court ruled against Gould, declaring that "a lease made by the husband during coverture, of land held in right of his wife, of which she had been endowed in consequence of a prior marriage, cannot enure against the woman after a divorce." The court then went on to make a more sweeping decree: "The Court consider the operation of a divorce . . . to be, to restore to the woman her interest entire in all the real estate which the husband held in her right by the intermarriage, and which by their joint act had not been legally conveyed during the coverture." The Vermont court expressed the belief that while marriage "covered" a woman's right to own property, the dissolution of the marriage removed that covering and restored full property rights to the former wife.[34]

When compared with other states, Vermont's alimony practice was quite liberal. Many states' statutes posited the wife's innocence as a prerequisite for the return of her property and for an additional award of alimony. In New York, unless the wife was the aggrieved party and had conducted herself impeccably, her divorced husband might retain his marital rights to her property. Jurist Zephaniah Swift explained that in Connecticut, "On the divorce, the rights of the wife to her estate revive in the same manner as if the husband had died." However, if she had not brought property into the marriage, Connecticut statute dictated that a divorced woman retained her dower right to her husband's estate only if she was the innocent party. In contrast, the Vermont Supreme Court granted alimony to six women who appeared as defendants in divorce proceedings between 1790 and 1830.[35]

Unlike the Vermont court's fairly liberal alimony awards, Connecticut divorce settlements rarely granted property to women. Between 1790 and 1830, the Connecticut Superior Court heard 190 women's divorce petitions when sitting in Hartford County; in only two cases do the records indicate that the court awarded alimony.[36] Scattered evidence suggests that the Connecticut court did allow divorced women to reclaim property they had brought into their marriages, regardless of whether they were the aggrieved or the offending party. For example, shortly after she married Henry Bissell in 1814, Elizabeth Wolcott Bissell inherited a small plot of land in East Windsor. In 1822, Henry successfully petitioned for divorce on the grounds of desertion, claiming that Elizabeth had taken their only child when she left him in 1819. The divorce decree does not mention alimony or any other property distribution; however, when Elizabeth died in 1848, her will bequeathed the property she had inherited to her son and his wife.[37] Likewise, when Elizabeth Johnson petitioned for divorce in 1801, she requested that the court assign her as alimony a bequest from her father, who had recently died. The desire to retain access to her father's legacy appears to have motivated Johnson to seek the divorce, for she claimed in her petition that her husband "threatens to take, appropriate, and dispose of [the bequest] to his own use." The court granted her petition for divorce but did not mention alimony. It is likely, however, that Elizabeth Johnson did receive her father's bequest, as she appears as an independent head of household on a subsequent census.[38] Bissell's and Johnson's stories indicate that divorce restored the property that Connecticut women had brought into their marriages; however, the Connecticut court appears to have been unwilling to grant additional alimony awards. The Connecticut Assembly was more generous, awarding alimony to 55 percent of women who requested it. Unless a woman had brought property into the marriage, however, the legislature only granted cash awards (which were difficult to enforce) and use rights to former husbands' real property.[39]

The Connecticut court's conservatism on married women's property extended beyond its unwillingness to grant alimony awards. In 1790, the Connecticut Superior Court reversed a lower court decision in favor of Bethiah Kinsman, widow of Robert Kinsman. During Robert's life, Jeremiah Kinsman had leased a piece of property to Robert and Bethiah, for the term of their natural lives. Robert died shortly after sowing rye on the leased land; his will appointed Jeremiah executor of his estate and bequeathed all his personal property and a cash annuity to Bethiah. When Jeremiah cut the rye that had grown on the leased property, Bethiah successfully sued him in the county court on trespassing charges. However, on appeal, the superior court found for Jeremiah, explaining that because the rye had not been severed from the land, "it did not pass by the bequest of personal estate" to Bethiah. The court acknowledged that Bethiah had an estate for life in the leased property; however, it refused to grant her any role in the management of that estate. Uncomfortable with granting a woman control over real property, the court upheld the executor's authority.[40]

In 1804, the Connecticut Supreme Court of Errors heard another case that pitted a widow against an executor. Marylynn Salmon has analyzed this case in her study of property law in early America; however, it bears mention here because of what the case reveals about the Connecticut court's attitudes towards married women's property.[41] Mary and Samuel Hutton had owned a piece of land in common, which Samuel sold, after Mary's consent was secured by his "repeated and importunate intreaties [sic]" and his promise that Mary could keep the money from her share of the land "for her sole, and separate Use." Samuel gave Mary notes from the buyer for the amount of her share, which she put away. Upon

Samuel's death, his executor took the notes from Mary, redeemed them, and then refused to give the money to Mary, who appealed to the court, saying "she has not in any way been satisfied for her Land." Mary had successfully negotiated with her husband to receive her fair share of the proceeds of the property sale; however, the Connecticut court refused to recognize the validity of this negotiation. The court explained that "by the Common Law the Husband and Wife are considered as one person in Law . . . as a Consequence of this Union of Persons, the principles necessarily result, and have been established, that Husband and Wife cannot Contract with each other." The court refused to recognize Samuel and Mary Hutton's agreement securing Mary an equitable share from the sale of her own property. According to the Connecticut court, once a woman gave her husband permission to sell land in which she held an interest, she had no right to the proceeds of the sale apart from what she might eventually receive as dower or a bequest. To acknowledge the legitimacy of Mary and Samuel Hutton's agreement would be to acknowledge that husbands and wives could have separate interests, a possibility the common law denied.[42]

The Connecticut court's conservatism reflected its concern with preserving legal doctrines regarding the unity of husband and wife. In 1805, the court declared that "the harmony and good order of society result naturally from peace and harmony in families, which will nowhere be found, without an entire union of interests between husband and wife." The court claimed that in England, so many special trust and prenuptial agreements had secured property "to the independent use of the wife" that "very little property, belonging to females, remains subject to the general law of coverture." According to the court, this state of affairs had resulted in numerous separation agreements. However, in Connecticut,

No property has been settled on a female, to her sole and separate use, independent of her husband. To the honor of females, in this state, they have despised the idea of with-holding their property from a man, with whom they would trust their persons. . . . The consequence has been, that no articles of separation have appeared, and but one divorce *a mensa et thoro* ever heard of, in the state. A comment cannot be necessary, to show the impropriety of adopting principles, tending to establish interests, views and prospects, in married women, independent of, and distinct from their husbands.

From the Connecticut court's perspective, acknowledging married women's right to own and control property inevitably would create separate interests and conflicts between husbands and wives, conflicts that could tear apart families and threaten social stability. Even when couples such as Samuel and Mary Hutton successfully negotiated these conflicts, the Connecticut court refused to acknowledge that wives legally could act as independent individuals who held separate interests.[43]

Mary and Samuel Hutton's negotiation over the sale of their land reveals a lived experience that contradicted the dictates of the common law, which insisted that women were economically dependent on men and that wives could not have interests that were separate from their husbands. This contradiction between lived experience and legal doctrine existed alongside different interpretations of the common law found in different states. In some jurisdictions, such as Vermont, the courts acknowledged women's right to family property *after* their marriages had ended. In jurisdictions such as Connecticut, the courts were more reluctant to allow women's ownership and control of family property even once the women were no longer married. This variability in New England courts' application of the common law and the competing claims of husbands and wives regarding women's labor and property ownership point to the unsettled nature of married women's economic status. As the New England economy shifted toward production for the market, and as households' consumer spending increased, the nature and meaning of women's work began to change. Although production for and consumption in the market heightened the importance of women's household work, at the end of the eighteenth and in the early decades of the nineteenth centuries, an ideology that obscured women's labor emerged. Elopement notices bear witness to New England wives' attempt to retain a measure of control over their labor and to struggle against this new characterization of their work. Women's ability to obtain divorces and alimony grants in some states, and their willingness to challenge their husbands' interpretation of their economic contributions in word and in deed reveal the contested nature of wives' status. While husbands emphasized their wives' consumer activities and their own status as economic providers, married women forcefully proclaimed the importance of their contributions to household economic survival and claimed to be partners with, not dependents of, their husbands.

4

"The Wicked Agency of Others"

Community Involvement and Marital Discord

On November 26, 1803, John Bolton placed an advertisement in the Danville *North Star*:

> By the Malicious representations and advice of evil disposed persons, on the 11th day October last, Cynthia my wife was induced without my knowledge, to quit my family. Having endeavored to persuade her to return and assured her of my willingness to support and treat her as an affectionate Husband—My own safety compels me, since she continues absent and adheres to the advice of those whom she may consider as friends, to caution the Public against giving her Credit on my account, as I am determined to pay no debts of her contracting.

Bolton's notice reveals a recurring theme running through the advertisements and experiences of New England couples coping with marital conflict in the early national period: the involvement of the community in couples' most intimate affairs. Although Bolton did not reveal the particular issues that caused the couple's difficulties, it is clear that Cynthia had discussed their marital problems with her neighbors and friends and that John Bolton believed that these "evil disposed persons" had convinced Cynthia to leave him. During the six weeks between Cynthia's elopement and the appearance of her husband's notice, John Bolton and other community members vied with one another for influence over Cynthia. John "endeavored to persuade her to return," while Cynthia's friends urged her to remain separated from her husband. Only when John was certain that Cynthia had decided to follow "the advice of those whom she may consider as friends" did he alert the larger community beyond the couple's immediate acquaintances of his wife's desertion and his refusal to allow her access to his credit. John Bolton clearly did not appreciate the nature of the advice that community members gave to his wife. However, the fact that he revealed the couple's difficulties to the entire readership of Danville's only newspaper indicates that Bolton recognized and accepted as normal community interference in marital relationships.[1]

Historians recognize that contemporary notions of family and marital privacy do not apply to the domestic relations of Americans in the colonial and early national eras. Scholars such as Nancy Cott and Hendrik Hartog have stressed the role that the "public," or local community, played in legitimizing early American marriages and enforcing appropriate standards of behavior for both spouses. In cases of marital conflict, couples' neighbors, friends, and families were the first to judge whether husbands and wives had fulfilled the obligations of the marriage contract. When husbands and wives placed elopement notices, they crafted their claims to meet prevailing community understandings regarding husbands' and wives' responsibilities and rights. As a result, the words these couples used to describe their marriages and the ways in which communities responded to these marital crises provide a glimpse into the way New Englanders perceived and acted upon the often ambiguous and contradictory features of common law marriage.[2]

Like John Bolton, husbands and wives often revealed that community members had interfered in their conflicts long before they printed their notices. In 1805, William Wheeler blamed his marital difficulties on his wife Elizabeth, who "hath suffered herself to be dictated by, and to follow the directions of her good friends, who, for a long time have possessed a pretty heavy share of antipathy towards me." Likewise, Timothy Harris blamed his wife's desertion on "the evil enticement of corrupt advisers," and Joseph Root maintained that "undue influence from prejudiced persons and bad advisers" had convinced his wife to leave him. When Parker Chapy printed a notice restoring his wife's access to his credit, he explained that "by bad advice of one of my neighbors, I was the cause of forbidding any person to harbor or to trust my wife on my account, which was injurious and unjust." Blaming friends and neighbors for their marital discord may have been a convenient way for husbands and wives to deflect blame for their problems onto others; however, couples only resorted to such claims because they conformed to real social experience.[3]

Moses Bailey humorously referred to the interest that community members took in their neighbors' marital difficulties. After denying his estranged wife credit, he added,

> some of our Old-Fashioned neighbors say, That it is a shame for us to quarrel in our Old Age, and that we ought to bear in mind the covenant of God—and cleave fast to the guide of our youth (and all such stuff). But I think the jolly part of our Community, all the young sensible people, seem to agree that it is nonsense for two old Stocks to keep any longer together, 30 or 40 years is long enough! Besides, Neighbors want to have something to talk about, when they meet together in the long winter evenings. All our relations too, far and near, who take the Newspapers, will hear from us—and it is some honor to be in the newspapers; and as we are too old now to go far abroad to the wars, it is certainly best for people of spirit, to keep up something in imitation of it at home.

Bailey demonstrated a keen awareness of the audience that he intended his notice to reach. He acknowledged the role that neighbors and other community members had played in his marital difficulties. He also assumed the community's continued interest in his conflict with his wife. Bailey knew that readers would recognize themselves in his characterizations of "Old-Fashioned neighbors" and the "jolly part" of the community. He commented on neighbors spending winter evenings gossiping about others' marital problems and claimed that even distant relations would take special interest in his difficulties. Although Bailey wrote in jest of this intense community interest in the affairs of others, he took for granted its existence.[4]

Couples used elopement notices to undermine community support for the offending spouse and to rally public opinion around the aggrieved author. In his 1815 notice, Jonathan Smith wrote that his wife, Hannah, "by her unbecoming conduct, has justly merited the disapprobation of the public, by her undutiful behavior and by the expense she has incurred to me." Smith intended his notice to notify merchants that he no longer would be responsible for his wife's debts. However, he also may have hoped that "the disapprobation of the public" would convince his wife to return and behave appropriately. Husbands and wives who printed notices vied for community support through the medium of the local newspaper because that support could manifest itself in concrete ways. Community members could serve as witnesses in divorce proceedings. Notices could try to persuade town officials to grant poor relief to estranged wives. Neighbors and friends might pressure an offending spouse to reconcile and fulfill his or her duties, or they could provide shelter and financial assistance to wives experiencing marital difficulties.[5]

Ruth Austin of Suffield, Connecticut, responded to her husband Nathaniel's notice by blaming her marriage troubles on the interference of Nathaniel's nephew and several other community members. Austin closed her notice with an appeal to the judgment of her community: "This town is the place of my nativity, where I am known, and I am perfectly willing that the public should enquire into my character, and see if I am such a Woman as I am represented to be." At least one member of Austin's community rose to her defense and wrote a lengthy letter to the *Impartial Herald,* Suffield's only newspaper. The author confirmed Ruth's account of her marital conflict and claimed that "Mrs. A. was born and bro't up in this place, where the goodness of her character is firmly established, and has always lived in peace and quietness with all her friends and neighbors." Although the records do not reveal how the residents of Suffield responded to these pleas on Ruth Austin's behalf, these and other notices reveal couples' belief that securing community support was vital to resolving their marital difficulties.[6]

Husbands and wives who posted advertisements employed distinctly gendered strategies in their attempts to sway the opinions of community members. Both men and women attempted to damage their spouses' reputations, but in markedly different ways. Every husband's notice, regardless of whether or not it contained details of a wife's inappropriate behavior, called the woman's sexual fidelity into question. Desertion postings highlighted runaway wives' inability to support themselves. Because women were legally dependent on men for their maintenance, the notices implied that if a woman was not receiving support from her husband, she must be receiving it from another man, presumably in an adulterous context. Indeed, legal commentators generally assumed that wives who eloped had left their husbands to live with other men. Some men included specific charges of sexual misconduct in their notices. John Severans declared his wife Abigail "guilty of the heinous crime of Adultery," while Herba Child lamented that his wife Molly had "gone away with another man." Homes Greenwood claimed that his wife Mary, "by her great fondness of variety, has broken her marriage covenant." Other husbands described their wives' behavior in language that suggested adulterous behavior without explicitly accusing their wives of any illicit activity. Moses Allard complained that his wife Lydia refused to behave "as the principles of virtue require," and Robert Dickey claimed his wife had "behaved herself very indecently." Both Parson Greenwood and William Andrews accused their wives of behaving "in a most scandalous manner."[7]

Gossip regarding the sexual behavior of estranged wives was inevitable, even when their husbands had not accused the women of adultery. In April 1799, George Cunningham reported his wife Delia's elopement in the *Rutland Herald*. Cunningham's notice included no details; he merely stated that Delia had left him and that he would no longer pay her debts. Rumors about Delia's illicit sexual activities abounded, however, and three weeks after the publication of her husband's notice, an advertisement signed by Ezekial Porter appeared in the *Herald*: "To Whom it concerns, this certifies, that I do not know that Delia Cunningham has the venereal disease, or that she ever had it, or what it [sic] is called the French Pox." Ezekial Porter's relation to the Cunninghams is a mystery. He probably was a neighbor who, in order to protect himself from a slander suit, felt obliged to deny having started a rumor. Porter's notice confirms that marital separations elicited community interest and participation in the form of rumors about the couple in question. Printing an elopement notice alerted more community members to a couple's difficulties and therefore added to the gossip surrounding the separation. His posting also confirms estranged wives' vulnerability to charges of illicit sexual activity.[8]

Wives also complained of their husbands' sexual misbehavior, but they were more apt to use their notices to cast doubts on their spouses' financial standing in the community.[9] Thankful Hutchens accused her husband of being a "fortune hunter," and claimed that "I have never heard that any body owed him a debt, if they do, they had better pay him immediately, as he will want it, for I shall maintain him no longer." Mehitabel Tylor claimed that her husband Job "is very fond of trading, by which means he has reduced himself and family to a state of want." Such wives far outnumbered women like Lois Vaughan, who lamented that her husband "has embraced the bosoms of strange women."[10]

Women who placed advertisements knew that it was important for men to maintain good credit in their communities. They were aware that their position as wives conferred on them influence over community perceptions of their husbands' credit and presented them with opportunities to cast their husbands' financial reputations in a negative light. These women also knew that the law obligated husbands to provide economic support for their wives. Information regarding their husbands' inability or refusal to provide such support would increase wives' chances of obtaining poor relief and, if necessary, a divorce. Estranged wives were eligible for poor relief only if they could convince overseers of the poor that they had not provoked their marital conflicts. If an eloped woman could present herself as a dutiful, faithful wife whose husband had neglected her, the town could charge the husband for any relief provided to his wife. Likewise, because a husband's absence alone was not considered evidence of his desertion, a woman who wished to divorce her husband on these grounds needed to prove that he had not provided her with economic support.[11]

New England wives often attacked with relish their husbands' status as economic providers. Lucy Thayer informed the public that her husband David "has lately taken the poor man's oath on the small sum of seven bushels of ashes; and I have not been able for years to obtain one cent on my dear husband's credit." Polly Ann Bulkly reported that "it was well understood in the vicinity of his [her husband John's] residence, that if he really possesses the credit for which his solicitude is now so great, those who know him best have not been yet so fortunate as to arrive at any knowledge of the circumstances." Clarissa Post also mocked the concern for his credit that her husband had expressed in his notice when she wrote "that nobody would harbor, or trust, me one cent on his account" because of her husband's inability to support himself. These wives understood that although they had no legal power to deprive their husbands of access to their credit, they could influence public opinion and gain significant advantages by casting doubts on their spouses' economic abilities.[12]

Unlike Polly Ann Bulkly and Clarissa Post, the overwhelming majority of women involved in these marital conflicts did not post notices detailing their sides of their marital difficulties. Why did so few wives place notices in newspapers? Unlike their husbands, wives did not have to protect their credit with merchants; still, printing notices could bring estranged wives legal benefits in divorce proceedings or petitions for poor relief. In spite of these incentives, between 1790 and 1830, women wrote less than 5 percent of elopement notices appearing in Vermont newspapers and less than 3 percent of Connecticut newspaper postings. In part, this vast disproportion between the number of men's and women's notices reflects prevailing social norms that discouraged women from deliberately exposing themselves to public scrutiny. Women who chose to defend themselves in print against their husbands' accusations recognized that they ran the risk of losing support from community members by drawing further attention to themselves in such a public manner.

In spite of the vigor with which female notice authors attacked their husbands' actions and reputations, wives who wrote advertisements often included disclaimers justifying their presence in a public forum. Esther Woodbury began her notice by stating, "It is with reluctance that I trouble the public with these lines; but in vindication of my character, I think it my duty to do it." Sally Meigs explained that after reading her husband's advertisement, "reason forbids that I should suffer such infamous aspersions to pass unnoticed." She placed her own advertisement "in vindication of my innocence." Likewise, Hester Smith claimed that because her husband had "aspersed my character and posted me in the public paper, I think it my duty to make the abuse I have received from him alike public." These wives knew that the members of their communities did not readily accept women's voices in the public sphere; therefore, they had to appear reluctant to approach the public with their versions of events. Such wives blamed their husbands for focusing the public's attention on them; they claimed that they were forced to respond publicly to protect their reputations. Wives who addressed the public without apparent hesitation ran the risk of confirming their husbands' accusations of headstrong or inappropriate behavior, and this may have influenced their decision not to respond publicly to their husbands' notices.[13]

For some estranged wives, shielding themselves from public scrutiny was the best way to safeguard their reputations. However, the difference in frequency with which men and women posted advertisements also reflects the different limits of their social worlds. Women's social and business circles typically were smaller than men's. Although elopement notices reveal that wives did do business with merchants, artisans, and other community members, their daily household duties usually kept them at home and limited their contacts to neighbors and family members. Men's commercial activities, such as marketing their produce, and their participation in civic activities, such as town meetings and election days, brought them into contact with a greater number and wider range of people. When couples experienced marital difficulties, wives could explain their sides of their conflicts to neighbors and family members—the people to whom they would turn for assistance—without placing advertisements in newspapers. Although close neighbors, friends, and family members might be familiar with both spouses' complaints and behavior, husbands often needed to influence opinions beyond this circle of intimates. Husbands had to ensure that those in their more extensive commercial and social networks continued to hold their credit and reputations in high regard. In order to reach all the members of their networks, men had to resort to placing elopement notices in newspapers.[14]

Men's advertisements reveal that many wives effectively used oral networks to defend themselves and to spread rumors about their husbands' behavior and character. Jeremiah Richardson justified denying his wife credit because "she and others of her connections had slandered my good name." Titus Burr claimed that his wife Elizabeth intended her "false reports . . . to injure me all she can." James Bacon accused his wife of having "been the means of injuring my property and character," echoing Rueben Hosmer, who maintained that his wife had said "many things injurious to my character and interest." Notices such as these attest to the power of women's personal connections. A wife who spread rumors of her husband's inappropriate conduct or imprudent habits could ruin a man's credit as easily as one who contracted excessive debts. These husbands hoped to restore their damaged credit and reputations by publicly discrediting their wives' actions and words.[15]

Husbands' attempts to cast doubt on their wives' versions of events also reveal that community members often were involved in crafting the notices. Along with blaming their marital difficulties on the interference of neighbors and friends, some husbands claimed that their wives were not the actual authors of their advertisements, but that the women had merely signed notices that others had prepared. In 1820, Isaac Danforth posted an advertisement accusing his wife Susan of deserting. Susan responded in print, claiming that she had left her husband because of his intolerable severity. Several weeks later, Isaac Danforth posted another advertisement, claiming that several of his male neighbors had written the notice that appeared in Susan's name. Danforth accused these neighbors of "creating and continuing a separation of my family" and asked, "Why should they hold out the arguments they did, to persuade my wife to sign what she and they knew was false?" Likewise, Aaron Colton of Hartford, Connecticut, claimed that his marital problems were the result of a "malicious scribbler who had the audacity to write" a notice designed to appear as if it had been written by Colton's wife, Rebecca.[16]

Husbands' efforts to undermine their wives' credibility in this way do not necessarily impugn these women's accounts. However, women themselves sometimes confirmed their husbands' accusations by admitting that they had not written their advertisements. In 1805, James Pell posted a notice claiming that his wife, Abigail, had "been enticed, by some evil minded persons, to leave my bed and board." Abigail responded with a lengthy notice, in which she detailed her husband's abuse and claimed that she had left James because she could no longer "live in such fear and imminent danger." However, slightly more than one month later, Abigail posted another advertisement:

> I hereby certify, that the advertisement which I caused to be published . . . respecting my husband, James Pell, was done without consideration, and is without foundation; it being drawn by another person, and not sufficiently examined by me, before I sent the same, and I hope no person will think any worse of the said James, in consequence of the said advertisement, being myself heartily sorry that I was in any respect, the cause of such an instrument.

Abigail Pell was not alone in blaming the influence of others for her words and actions. In her response to her husband's notice, Rebecca Read claimed "that I never had thoughts of leaving him until we were advised to part, by some friends." Likewise, in January of 1812, Belinda Smalley of Middlebury, Vermont, posted a notice in which she explained that several months earlier she had petitioned the supreme court

> for a bill of divorcement from my husband, Zera Smalley, but being at that time in a low state of health and my mind somewhat deranged, and also being wrongly informed and advised by my mother, and other unfriendly people. I do therefore freely say that I had no just provocation for such a publication, and am thoroughly convinced that the reports concerning him were made by designing and malicious persons with an intent to injure him and myself. It is therefore my sincere wish and request, that the said petition be of no effect or virtue, & that nothing further be done about it.

Postings such as these make it clear that, for some wives, notice authorship was a collaborative process that ranged from signing notices that others had written to incorporating neighbors', family members', and friends' suggestions and complaints into their advertisements.[17]

Other evidence indicates that husbands' postings were created collaboratively at least as often as were wives' notices. Husbands sometimes copied unusual phrases from other men's notices when constructing their own postings, a process that printers may have encouraged by providing husbands with standard formats for their advertisements. For example, on March 30, 1801, the *Connecticut Courant* printed an advertisement signed by Isaac Case, claiming that his wife Elizabeth "has for a long time behaved in a very unbecoming manner, and in defiance of the best advice, has of late absconded from me." Approximately six weeks later, the same paper printed Ebenezer Couch's notice claiming that *his* wife "has for a long time behaved in a very unbecoming manner, and in defiance of the best advice, has of late absconded from me." The same unique, word-for-word phrasing reappeared nearly three years later in an advertisement signed by Joseph Steel. Perhaps Ebenezer Couch and Joseph Steel felt that Isaac Case's words aptly described their experience, or perhaps the printer of the *Courant* used Case's notice as a convenient model. The editorial hand of newspaper printers also is visible in notices that appeared one week with spelling mistakes that were then corrected in the following week's issue. Other notices reveal that some printers simply inserted appropriate names into standard notices, a practice that could cause embarrassment when the printer inserted the wrong name. On January 9, 1809, a notice appeared in the Bennington *World* in which Benjamin Griffis accused his wife "Mary" of desertion. One week later, the same announcement appeared with the name "Mercy" inserted. Griffis's wife, whose real name was Mercy, took advantage of this error and posted her own notice, stating, "Whereas Benjamin Griffis has advertised his wife *Mary*—I, Mercy, his wife, forbid his ever advertising me with the charge he did *Mary*, for I am not guilty of it." Interestingly, the printer felt obliged to add a postscript to Mercy's notice, explaining that "the Printer made the error, and corrected it."[18]

The printer's attempt to protect Benjamin Griffis from embarrassment is particularly revealing. In spite of evidence that suggests that *both* men and women created their notices collaboratively, men were far more likely to raise the issue of notice authorship to undermine their spouses' credibility. Only one New England woman attempted to cast doubt on the authorship of her husband's posting.[19] Men appear to have been less vulnerable than women to the charge that they had not authored their notices. After all, when Mercy Griffis poked fun at the mistake in her husband's notice, the joke depended on readers believing that Benjamin had written the notice and made the mistake himself. By claiming responsibility for the error, the printer inadvertently revealed the collaborative nature of many notices. Yet, doubts regarding authorship appear to have been most convincing when men raised them about women's advertisements.

A growing body of scholarship analyzing the role of gender in the early republic offers a possible interpretive framework within which to situate this intersection of marital conflict, gender, and authorship. Scholars such as Jan Lewis, Joan Gunderson, and Nancy Isenberg have demonstrated that the male citizens of the new nation defined republican citizenship in language that drew heightened attention to perceived differences between men and women. Americans in the early national period believed that only male citizens were capable of independent judgment and action. Because of their legal subordination to their husbands, married women were dependents who relied on their husbands to provide for them economically and to represent their interests in the political sphere. According to this gendered paradigm, there was little possibility that married women could exercise independent judgment and action, a belief that rendered women more vulnerable than men to the charge that words published in their names were not truly their own. The one New England woman who claimed that her husband had not authored the notice that appeared in his name described her spouse as a person "who is not so much acquainted with the world of mankind as [are] people in general." Ruth Austin had to attempt to convince readers that her husband was more naïve and gullible than the typical man before she could accuse him of publishing a notice others had written. Her charge ran counter to norms regarding masculine independence; as a result, she tried to explain why these prevailing norms did not apply to her husband. It was unnecessary for husbands to offer such explanations, because a man's charge that his wife had not authored a posting that appeared in her name resonated with existing cultural beliefs regarding women's dependence and vulnerability.[20]

The evidence suggests that some couples raised issues of notice authorship in order to pave the way toward a reconciliation. When husbands publicly expressed doubts regarding the authorship of their wives' notices they provided their spouses with a way to shift the blame for their words and actions on to neighbors and family members. When Abigail

Pell claimed that her original notice accusing her husband of cruel treatment had been "drawn by another person, and not sufficiently examined by me," she was relying on her readers' willingness to believe that it was not only possible, but likely, that a woman could be persuaded to sign a notice that she had not written. Likewise, when Belinda Smalley explained that she had based her actions on reports about her husband that "were made by designing and malicious persons with an intent to injure him and myself," she was both clearing her husband of the charges she had levied against him and shielding herself from criticism by hiding behind accepted notions of women's dependence and vulnerability, and accepted norms of community interference in marriages.[21]

The involvement of neighbors and friends in couples' difficulties was commonplace; however, marital conflict sometimes could precipitate quite formal community interference in a couple's affairs. The financial interests of towns and villages dictated that local officials watch for signs of marital discord among community members. Wives who lost access to their husbands' credit might apply for poor relief and become chargeable to the town. Town officials were responsible for ensuring that marital conflict did not increase taxpayers' financial burdens. In October 1796, Jacob Lindsly of Bristol, Connecticut, denied his wife Mindwell access to his credit, claiming that she was "disposed unnecessarily to contract Debts on my account." He did not accuse Mindwell of desertion; rather, the root of the couple's difficulties appears to have been Jacob's unwillingness or inability to provide for his family. Anxious to avoid placing Mindwell Lindsly and the couple's children on the poor rolls, town officials pressured Jacob to support his family. In February 1797, Jacob deeded eighty acres of land with a dwelling house and barn to the town. After specifying the metes and bounds of the property, the deed continued:

> the condition of the within Deed is such that if the within Named Jacob Lindsly shall forever save the town of Bristol . . . from any Cost or Expense that may arise from the Support or maintenance of himself or his wife & Family that the within Deed to be void and of no effect but in Default thereof to Stay and remain in full force.

Town officials resorted to extraordinary measures to force Jacob Lindsly to support his wife and family. If he did not do so, he would lose his property. The town's coercive measures appear to have worked: in September

1808, the town deeded the property back to Lindsly as a result of his fulfillment of his obligations to his family. When Jacob Lindsly died in 1810, his estate was valued at over twenty-five hundred dollars. His will provided legacies for his six children and his wife. By interfering with the Lindsly's marriage difficulties, the town of Bristol helped ensure the family's support, as well as the stable, orderly transmission of property from one generation to the next.[22]

Town officers had a number of options available to protect their towns from financial liability when couples separated. At times, officials warned estranged couples out of town to prevent them from receiving poor relief, as did the selectmen of Dummerston, Vermont, when Luke and Rhody Graham separated. Town officials also could place quarreling couples and their children under public guardianship, a method that the selectmen of Pomfret, Vermont, used when Elisha and Jerusha Hutchinson experienced difficulties. The root of the Hutchinsons' troubles appears to have been Elisha's lack of economic success. In 1784 the Reverend Elisha Hutchinson was ordained the first settled minister of Pomfret's Congregational Church, and he served until dismissed in January of 1795. Hutchinson did not believe that the congregation had fulfilled its obligations toward him and, in May 1797, he sued the church for one thousand pounds in back wages. The jury found for the church, a decision that appears to have placed the Hutchinsons in difficult economic circumstances. One month later Hutchinson sold all the land he owned in Pomfret, but the proceeds of the sale were not enough to provide for his family and pay his debts. At the September 1797 session of the county court, Hutchinson was unable to pay the amount in damages that the court awarded to his creditors.[23]

These economic difficulties evidently placed a strain on the Hutchinsons' marriage. On October 13, 1797, Elisha denied his wife access to his credit, explaining that Jerusha "has for some time refused to bed with me, or to perform any duties to me which are incumbent upon her, and . . . she endeavors by many ways to injure my interest." Jerusha printed a response to her husband's accusations in which she claimed that Elisha's "complaints are absolutely false, and I can make it appear by sufficient witness." Jerusha did not mention that she had given birth to the couple's sixth child one month earlier, a circumstance that could account for Elisha's complaints and that also might have exacerbated the family's financial difficulties.[24]

The marital quarrel of this landless, unemployed man with six children drew the attention of Pomfret officials. On November 10, 1797, the selectmen placed a notice in the *Vermont Journal*:

> We, the subscribers being selectmen for the town of Pomfret for the time being, taking into consideration the situation of Elisha Hutchinson, and his family, respecting worldly affairs, and in our opinion it is needful that we do appoint an overseer to advise and direct Mr. Elisha Hutchinson in his business—and we do hereby, by the authority invested in us, appoint Henry Ainsworth as an overseer to advise and direct as above written, for the space of six months from the date of this instrument. And all persons are forbid trading or making any bargain with the said Elisha Hutchinson, without the leave of the said overseer, until the above term.[25]

Elisha Hutchinson's original advertisement was an attempt to shift the blame for his economic difficulties to his wife. Perhaps he intended his notice to persuade community officials that he was able to restore financial stability within his family. Jerusha's public response may have undermined her husband's attempt to convince the Pomfret selectmen that he had sufficient authority within his household to restore financial order. Ironically, Elisha Hutchinson's attempt to deprive his wife of her access to his credit helped bring about his own economic disempowerment.

Not surprisingly, a couple's economic status was paramount in determining whether and how local officials would interfere in marriage conflicts. When husbands had access to resources, town officials could pressure them to support their wives and families, as was the case with the Lindsly family. In contrast, at the time of the Hutchinsons' marital difficulties, their economic circumstances were uncertain, at best. Such troubled couples without access to economic resources posed a threat to town finances, and officials could move quickly to minimize their towns' financial responsibility for estranged couples and their families.

Occasionally, separated couples deliberately sought out formal community intervention. Isaac and Susan Danforth's difficulties reveal the gendered ways that husbands and wives used the law and the community to help them resolve their conflicts. On July 18, 1820, Dr. Isaac Danforth of Barnard, Vermont, advertised his wife's elopement. Danforth merely stated that Susan "has gone to parts unknown to me" and that she refused to return. Several weeks later Susan responded, explaining, "I think it a duty I owe to my friends, the public, and myself, to state to the public the causes that compelled me to leave his house, and to flee from his presence." She accused Isaac of having treated her with intolerable severity "in instances too numerous to mention." Susan also claimed that Isaac followed her when she left his home, took her clothing away, and threatened to carry off their children: Betsey, aged two, and Edward, six months.[26]

Over the course of the next three months, Isaac and Susan engaged in a debate via the *Woodstock Observer* regarding the causes of their conflict and their conduct since the separation. Public records and the couple's advertisements demonstrate that as the community's involvement shifted from the local level of friends, neighbors, and town officials to the county and state courts, Isaac and Susan moved from a position of relative equality before the community to one that privileged Isaac's version of events and denied Susan the opportunity to speak on her own behalf.

Isaac responded to Susan's advertisement on September 19 by blaming the couple's difficulties on the interference of neighbors. Danforth claimed that three men—Asa Briggs, Gardner Winslow, and Ebenezer Winslow—had helped his wife leave his home and were sheltering Susan and the couple's children. Isaac stated, "I am persuaded it is by the advice of Briggs and several women, that my wife has not returned to her home." Danforth attempted to portray all of the couple's difficulties as the product of their neighbor's machinations: "Thus has this unhappy affair, which originated in *less than nothing*, been carried on by the wicked agency of others, under the pretence that they were her friends." As noted previously, Isaac claimed that Susan had told him that Asa Briggs and Gardner Winslow had written the notice that had appeared in her name. He also accused the men of persuading Susan to apply for public relief rather than return to him.[27]

Danforth's version of events is striking for the lack of agency he ascribed to Susan. Isaac Danforth preferred to contend publicly with other men. If he attacked his wife in print he might have lent credence to her claims of verbal and physical abuse. Because husbands were supposed to protect their weaker spouses, by claiming that his male neighbors were meddling in his marital affairs, Isaac Danforth could portray himself as a solicitous husband who only desired to free his wife from the undue influence of unscrupulous men.

Danforth recognized the value of community support, for in his second notice he included the affidavits of six neighbors and boarders, each of whom swore that he or she had "never known or heard of [Danforth] giving his wife any harsh treatment, or hard words, but have always thought that he used her well." Unfortunately for Isaac, Susan's supporters held more prestigious positions in the community. Four of the six people who spoke out on Isaac's behalf appear to have worked as servants in the Danforth household, while the men to whom Susan had turned for help were independent heads of households. Indeed, Ebenezer Winslow served as a justice of the peace and did not hesitate to use his position to advance Susan's cause. Susan's supporters summoned Barnard's grand jury, which issued a warrant for Isaac's arrest and trial for "abuse to his wife." No record survives of Isaac Danforth's trial before the justice of the peace's court, but Gardner Winslow published a response to Isaac's second notice in which he referred to Danforth's trial and conviction.[28]

Susan Danforth also published a response to her husband's second advertisement. She denied that either Briggs or the Winslows had written her first notice or that they had persuaded her to apply for poor relief. Susan asserted that all her actions—from leaving her husband to writing her first advertisement and applying for poor relief—were the results of her own decisions. Susan's second notice was an attempt to avoid being marginalized by her husband's attacks on the men to whom she had turned for support. Isaac had tried to transform his marital difficulties into a dispute with other male community members, and Susan responded by claiming full responsibility for her actions. Although Gardner Winslow printed a response to Isaac's advertisement, he did so to protect his own reputation, not Susan's. Winslow wrote that Danforth's advertisement "accuses me and others of endeavouring to create a separation of his family—which assertion is a palpable falsehood." Winslow's notice was an attempt to remove himself from the Danforths' public argument while Susan's second advertisement was an effort to reposition herself at the center of the conflict.[29]

In spite of Susan's attempt to claim responsibility for her actions, Isaac continued to portray the conflict as an issue between men. In his third (and final) advertisement, Isaac claimed that Asa Briggs and the Winslows had unfairly influenced his trial before the justice of the peace's court by choosing a biased jury and judge: "No *innocence* can secure the *accused,* if the *Judges* and *Jurors,* are chosen by the *accuser."* Isaac then explained how he planned to fight his wife's supporters: "I appealed to the County Court, where it will appear how *great* is the *crime*; who were the instigators of this prosecution, and for what purpose." Danforth scarcely acknowledged his wife's second advertisement, noting "I barely observe (and I am sorry to be obliged to do it) that she has sworn to *two stories* [regarding the authorship of her first notice] which are *totally different.*" Still reluctant to attack his wife publicly, Isaac remained more comfortable describing his legal efforts against her male supporters.[30]

At the Windsor County Court's September session, Isaac Danforth had initiated a suit against Asa Briggs. In December the court called Briggs to defend himself against Danforth's charge that he had kidnapped Susan, Betsey, and Edward Danforth. Isaac claimed one thousand dollars in damages as a result of Briggs's actions. The jury found Briggs guilty and awarded Danforth $750 and court costs. Briggs appealed to the state supreme court, which heard the case in August 1821. When Danforth and Briggs appeared before the state's highest court, however, they agreed that the justices should declare the case nonsuit. Danforth agreed to the non-suit because he had achieved the desired result with the county court action. Isaac Danforth did not want Asa Briggs's money; he wanted Briggs to stop supporting and sheltering his wife and children. The county court's guilty verdict persuaded Briggs that he no longer could afford to help Susan Danforth. Deprived of her neighbor's support, Susan had little choice but to come to terms with Isaac. The couple did not reconcile, but Isaac regained custody of his two children. Although no record of a divorce survives, Isaac remarried. He and his second wife had no children before Isaac died in 1828, when he was only thirty-five years old. His second wife, Celia, retained custody of Isaac's and Susan's children. Susan Danforth never remarried. The records do not reveal how she survived alone, but she lived until 1865, when she died in Springfield, Vermont, at the age of seventy-four.[31]

For one year of their married life, Isaac and Susan Danforth were the objects of intense community scrutiny and interference. Both husband and wife openly invited the involvement of neighbors and local officials. Isaac had superior legal resources, however, that helped him prevail despite Susan's position of relative equality in terms of access to community support. In fact, Susan appears to have secured a more sympathetic response from the people of Barnard. Indeed, her supporters wielded more local power than Isaac's friends, and they used their power to Susan's economic and legal advantage. When Isaac transformed his problems with his wife into a conflict with his male neighbors, however, he gained the advantage. After his initial notice accusing Susan of desertion, Isaac directed his attacks not at his wife but at her male supporters. This strategy allowed Isaac to sidestep Susan's charge of intolerable severity. It also offered him a way to defend his reputation honorably, by contending with his male equals, instead of attacking the woman whom he had sworn to support and protect. Isaac's insistence that his male neighbors had caused his problems also made it possible for him to pursue a satisfactory legal resolution to his difficulties. The only action he could have taken against Susan was to petition for divorce. In order to obtain a divorce on the grounds of desertion, Isaac would have had to wait the three years required by statute. He also may have feared that Susan's accusations of cruelty would prevent him from regaining custody of his children. A suit against Asa Briggs on the grounds of kidnapping offered Isaac a swifter, more favorable resolution to his marital difficulties.

The Danforths' unusually well-documented case offers a glimpse into the gendered patterns of marriage law and of communities' involvement in marital disputes. Community support for wives could not overcome husbands' legal advantages. Although both husbands and wives could call upon the power of the court to grant divorces, husbands had more legal options to enforce their will within their marriages. Any man who sheltered an estranged wife exposed himself to legal action. One commentator on the law maintained that "the court will never take away a wife from a friend to whom she has fled to escape the effects of [her husband's] brutality." However, the same commentator insisted that

> to justify interference to remove a man's wife from his house, the defendant is bound to show that she was abused, nor will the mere statement of the plaintiff's wife, that she was abused by her husband, without any proof of such abuse, be a justification for the defendant's advice to her to leave her husband. Whenever the wife is not justifiable in leaving her husband, he who knowingly and intentionally assists her in violating her duty is guilty of a wrong for which an action will lie.[32]

Although the Barnard jury and many community residents believed that Isaac Danforth had mistreated his wife, Asa Briggs was not able to persuade the county court that Susan Danforth had left Isaac because of his abusive behavior. It is impossible to determine how many estranged wives were unable to obtain community support because of the possibility of legal action against those who offered them assistance. As long as the law refused to recognize married women as independent actors, husbands like Isaac Danforth could continue to blame their wives' male supporters for their marital difficulties. The threat of legal action against those who helped estranged wives was a powerful tool that could turn community involvement to husbands' advantage.

The words and experiences of couples such as Isaac and Susan Danforth help reveal the roles that community members played in negotiating resolutions to marital conflicts. When a married couple experienced difficulties, neighbors and friends were the first to begin sorting out which spouse had or had not upheld the responsibilities of the marriage contract, while economic circumstances or a direct appeal from one or both spouses could involve community members beyond this inner circle. Each of these community members held his or her own understanding of the reciprocal obligations of the marriage contract, and each marital conflict could generate different interpretations of which spouse had violated that contract. Neighbors and friends participated in these conflicts by offering quarreling couples advice regarding what to do and what words to publish in newspapers to garner support from the larger community. The advertisements, as well as gossip, played an important role in influencing prevailing community opinions about these marital conflicts, opinions that could manifest themselves when communities pressured spouses to change their ways or when they offered shelter and economic assistance to estranged wives. The greater frequency with which husbands placed their versions of their conflicts before the public might suggest that they had the upper hand in influencing community opinion, and the story of Isaac and Susan Danforth demonstrates that even when estranged wives obtained significant community support, it did not shield them from their husbands' greater legal power. However, the notices reveal that women effectively used oral networks to gain support. More importantly, women's occasional newspaper postings served to remind communities that every husband's notice represented only one contested version of a couple's marriage difficulties.

5

"Having Confidence in Her Own Abilities"
Coping with Estrangement

In the *Vermont Journal* of April 28, 1790, David Read accused his wife Rebecca of eloping, and he refused to pay any debts that she contracted. On May 19, Rebecca responded, claiming that "I never had thoughts of leaving him until we were advised to part, by some friends, as it was supposed we never should live agreeably together; we accordingly parted, and that mutually: he engaging to pay me a certain sum annually for my support; which however, he has not done—but neglects it." David and Rebecca Read had been among the first settlers of the town of Ryegate, Vermont, arriving in 1774 and taking possession of two lots of uncleared land and two house lots. David Read was a prosperous settler and was active in civic affairs. He owned five seats in the Ryegate meeting house, served in the Vermont militia during the Revolution, and served as town constable in 1776. According to Ryegate's 1789 Grand List, Read's tax assessment was the tenth highest out of forty-four total taxpayers. In 1794, Read was the eighth largest landowner in town. Read's prosperity and civic accomplishments did not make him immune to marital conflict, however. After their separation in 1790, David and Rebecca lived apart, never reconciling. When Rebecca died in 1817, probate records reveal that her estate was worth $228, just enough to pay her debts. Clothing, linens, household utensils, and a few pieces of furniture made up the modest estate. Rebecca Read owned no real estate and the records do not reveal where or with whom she had lived. When David died in 1826, his estate included a twenty-acre farm, livestock, tools, furniture, utensils, and clothing. After claims against the estate were settled and administrative costs paid, the estate was worth approximately sixteen hundred dollars.[1]

The records confirm that David and Rebecca Read remained permanently separated until their deaths.[2] In contrast, John and Hester Smith of Burlington, Connecticut, reconciled after they separated in 1812. The couple had married in 1794; Hester had borne at least two daughters and one son by 1812, when John posted her desertion on December 22. Hester responded on January 5, claiming that she had left because "he has frequently abused me in the most reproachful language; has frequently struck me, without provocation, with his fists and with clubs; wrung my neck; frequently turned me out of doors, and told me never to enter his doors again, and fastened the door against me." By 1820, Hester *had* entered John's doors again; when John died intestate in 1822, Hester received her dower share in his estate, which was worth over $750.[3]

Why did some couples reconcile while others remained separated? No doubt intangible factors such as personality, and emotions such as love, hurt, and anger played their parts in determining the outcomes of these conflicts. However, an examination of the lives of one hundred Vermont and seventy-five Connecticut couples who posted elopement notices between 1790 and 1830 reveals more material considerations that helped determine how couples coped with marital difficulties. An analysis of the strategies that couples pursued and the outcomes of their conflicts demonstrates that while husbands continued to hold legal and economic power over their estranged wives, some married women were able to maneuver around their legal disabilities to construct lives that offered them a measure of independence. In particular, an examination of the lives of women who remained permanently separated from their husbands without divorcing offers further evidence of the interrelationship between the limitations and opportunities that married women confronted.

Newspaper notices, census and tax records, as well as birth, probate, and divorce records reveal the outcomes for 68 percent of Vermont couples and 56 percent of Connecticut couples in the sample population.[4] The outcomes in both states were strikingly similar. In Vermont, 35 percent of couples with known outcomes reconciled; 28 percent remained permanently separated with no evidence of divorce; and 37 percent went on to divorce. In Connecticut, 38 percent reconciled; 29 percent remained permanently separated with no evidence of divorce; and 33 percent divorced.[5] A comparison of the social and economic characteristics of couples who reconciled with those who did not reveals the extent to which wives' dependence shaped the options they could pursue when their marriages threatened to disintegrate. Legal and economic disabilities prevented most married women from living independent, self-supporting lives after their marriages had failed. Although a small number of women managed to support themselves while living apart from their husbands without divorcing, they remained dependent on their spouses, if only for the men's willingness to allow them some independence.

Although the types of evidence available for couples in each state differ, the primary factor that determined whether a couple reconciled or not was the extent to which the wife was economically and socially dependent on her husband. Vermont wives who did not reconcile with their husbands were younger than Vermont wives who returned to their husbands (see table 2). In both Vermont and Connecticut, couples who reconciled had been married for longer periods of time than those who remained apart (see table 3). When Freelove McIntash left her husband William, she was seventeen years old and had been married a little more than six months. In contrast, Elizabeth Ainsworth was forty-one when she left her husband Wyman, to whom she had been married for at least twenty years. The McIntashes never reconciled; Freelove returned to her parents' home and later remarried. However, Elizabeth Ainsworth returned to her husband's home, where she lived until her death in 1832. A forty-one-year-old woman who had been married twenty years would have faced greater psychological and emotional difficulties when ending her marriage than would a seventeen-year-old who had been married for six months. Age and length of marriage had practical effects as well: a younger woman could remarry more easily, and couples who had been married for shorter lengths of time would have had fewer children to support, making permanent separation or divorce easier.[6]

Access to property, and hence, the ability to support themselves, was another significant factor in determining the course of action estranged wives chose to follow. The available evidence is limited, but quite sugges-

TABLE 2
Vermont Wives' Age at Elopement[a]

	Average Age	Number of Women
All Elopements	30	24
Reconciliations	36	9
Permanent Separations	23	5
Divorces	29	7
Unknowns	28	3

[a] Unfortunately, I was able to find age data for only seven Connecticut wives, an insufficiently representative sample to include them.

TABLE 3
Length of Marriage before Elopement

	Average Length (in years)	No. of Couples
All Elopements	8.1	92
Reconciliations	12.5	16
Permanent Separations	5.2	16
Divorces	7.4	38
Unknowns	8.1	22

tive. Seven of the eight Vermont wives who owned real property before marrying, and six of the ten Connecticut wives who brought real property into their marriages did *not* reconcile. In Vermont, not one of the wives who reconciled with their husbands had owned land before they married.[7] The lack of property ownership highlighted wives' dependence on their husbands. Husbands' refusal to pay the debts of women without access to economic resources placed these wives in an extremely difficult situation. Without property with which to attempt to support themselves, wives more easily acquiesced to their husbands' demands and returned home. In contrast, wives who retained access to property they had brought into their marriages could use that property to obtain the economic support they normally would have received from their husbands. Betsey Paine of Woodstock, Vermont, inherited from her first husband lifetime use rights to half a farm and a house. When she and her second husband, Abel, separated, she retained possession of her former husband's property. In fact, it appears that Betsey and Abel Paine had lived on her first husband's farm and that in spite of his notice accusing Betsey of refusing to live with him, Abel was the one who had left. Similarly, when Thankful Hutchens of East Windsor, Connecticut, separated from her husband, Thomas, she continued to live in a house she had inherited before marrying. Although no record exists of a divorce, when Thankful Hutchens died, the probate court honored her will devising her property to various sisters, nieces, and nephews. Because of their access to property, wives such as Betsey Paine and Thankful Hutchens did not face the same economic pressure to return to their spouses that confronted other wives.[8]

Regardless of whether they reconciled or remained apart, couples rarely determined the fate of their marriages in a vacuum. Families played particularly significant roles in mediating couples' conflicts, and family members were an especially crucial source of support to wives who had left their husbands. When Esther Woodbury responded to her husband John's notice, she explained that "it was his ill treatment and hard threatenings that drove me from his house, and obliged me to apply to my parents for protection." Ranna Cossit accused the grown children from his wife Martha's first marriage of persuading her to leave him and assisting her in removing property from his house. When Job Tylor reported his wife Mehitable's desertion, he claimed that she had left with "a man by the name of Isaac Tukesbury, who she had been frequently with for four or five months previous to her departure." Tylor intended that his wife's liaison with Tukesbury appear illicit; however, the vast majority of community members no doubt knew that Isaac Tukesbury was one of Mehitable's three brothers. The presence of parents, adult children, and siblings was an important resource for wives experiencing marital difficulties. As well as offering emotional support, a woman's kin could provide for her economically. If a woman's parents, siblings, or children would take her in when she left her husband, she need not fear economic deprivation.[9]

In some cases, families could help couples come to terms and reconcile. Salmon Cogswell posted his wife Sarah's desertion in October of 1794. One month later he posted a retraction in which he acknowledged that Sarah had gone to her parents. He asked Sarah's forgiveness and assured her that "if she will return and live with me I will use her well in future." However, he only did so "after her father had assured me that if I would let her stay with her mother a few days I would not be put to a farthing cost nor run in debt any way." By agreeing to pay for the cost of Sarah's trip and by supporting her during her visit, Sarah's father made possible a reconciliation. Likewise, when Elam and Abigail Pease separated in 1819, family helped achieve a reconciliation. After Elam posted her desertion, Abigail responded by claiming that Elam was not supporting her, but that she had used property she had inherited from her father to pay his debts. The actions of Elam's and Abigail's eldest son saved their marriage by providing Elam with the means to support his wife. Their son leased a dwelling house and plot of land to his father in exchange for Elam's agreement "to maintain and support the said Abigail Pease, during her natural life." A lasting reconciliation was possible once their son ensured that Elam would support Abigail.[10]

These examples of family involvement demonstrate the importance of economic security for both husbands and wives. These couples' experiences reaffirm the importance of economic exchange to the marriage relationship and to marital conflict. Clearly, access to economic support played a crucial role in determining whether or not couples would reconcile. Wives without any source of support other than their husbands faced tremendous pressure to reconcile. It is difficult to determine how these wives fared when they returned to their husbands. Wives who reconciled virtually disappear from public records; their names appear only on birth records when the couples registered any children they had after the reconciliation, and in probate records when their husbands died. Roxalania Sanderson of Springfield, Vermont, eloped from her husband Amos in June of 1814, not quite two years after they had married. Amos Sanderson's name appears in Springfield land records after the desertion and on the federal census of 1820; however, the only clue that exists to Roxalania's fate is the presence of her name on the birth certificates of four children that she and Amos registered between 1815 and 1825. Rebecca Colton of Hartford, Connecticut, left her husband Aaron in September of 1817. Several weeks later Aaron posted a notice explaining that he and Rebecca had reconciled and restoring her access to his credit. Aaron Colton appears in numerous records after the couple's reconciliation. He is listed as a head of household in the 1820 census; he appears in county court records as a plaintiff or defendant in various debt cases; and he appears in the 1825 Hartford City Directory. After the reconciliation, however, Rebecca disappears from all records until Aaron's death in 1827, when the county court affirmed her appointment as guardian of the couple's two minor children. When a couple reconciled, wives' status as legal subordinates once again covered them from public view. They appear in records as adjuncts to their husbands, bearing the men's children and inheriting their share of the men's estates.[11]

Women who reconciled with their husbands did so, in part, for reasons of economic security. However, opportunities existed in Connecticut and Vermont for women to support themselves while remaining apart from their husbands. In particular, an examination of the lives of women who remained separated from their husbands without obtaining divorces offers a fascinating glimpse into the ways in which these women struggled to balance their dependent legal status with a day-to-day existence that sometimes provided them with opportunities to act independently. Wives who remained separated from their husbands appear in census, tax, land, and court records, in spite of the fact that, technically, they remained *femes covert*. Their presence in the public records makes it possible to determine the strategies that some wives who remained apart from their husbands pursued. Although the numbers are small, an analysis of these women's lives reveals the opportunities available to married women to act in their own interests, as well as the limitations with which they had to contend.

More than 40 percent of these women either relied on nearby kin for support or remarried without the benefit of divorce (see table 4).[12] Essentially, these wives survived by becoming dependents in the homes of men other than their husbands. While this strategy might appear to be exchanging one dependency for another, the women knew that dependent subordination was a negotiable status. Anna Norris responded to her husband's notice by informing him and the public that she had moved "to my father's to live . . . [because] there never was a person more abused than you have abused me." Norris believed that living as a dependent in her father's household was far preferable to holding the same status in her husband's home. Although dependence was a fixed legal status, couples had to negotiate the day-to-day meaning of a wife's subordination to her husband. Did a wife's legal status mean that she had to submit quietly to her husband's every decision, or did she play an active role in the decision-making process? Did dependence or partnership characterize a wife's economic relationship with her husband? Wives who deserted and became dependents in other men's homes were dissatisfied with the everyday implications of their subordination to their husbands. They believed that their fathers, brothers, or new husbands offered them more satisfactory situations.[13]

Estranged wives who did not remarry and who had no kin to whom they could turn for support had to find ways to support themselves. If they did not have access to any economic resources outside of their husbands' households, these women could turn to public relief, but only if they convinced local officials that they were the innocent party in their conflicts with their husbands. In order to get a sympathetic reception from poor-relief officials, an eloped wife had to present herself as the victim of her husband's cruelty or neglect. Only if she could prove to town officials that she had been dutiful and faithful would an estranged wife be eligible for poor relief. Public charity was the option of only the most desperate women, for it meant either residence in a poor house or being "auctioned off" to live and serve in the household of the person who offered to accept the lowest sum from the town for the pauper's board. Records indicate that only one wife from the sample population followed this route. Stephen Kimball of Middlebury, Vermont, advertised that his

TABLE 4
*Strategies of Wives Who Remained Permanently Separated
from Their Husbands without Divorcing*[a]

Strategy	Number	Percentage
Self-support (employment or property ownership)	8	47
Dependence on Male Kin or New Husband	7	41
Poor Relief	1	6
Other[b]	1	6

[a] I was able to determine the strategies of seventeen of the thirty-one Connecticut and Vermont wives who remained separated from their husbands without evidence of divorcing.

[b] Julia Thomas, whose case is discussed later in this chapter.

wife Esther had eloped in December of 1821. Esther retorted and claimed that he had turned her out of his home for no cause. Stephen later returned to his native New Hampshire and Esther turned to poor relief. When she died three decades later, she was still a pauper, dependent on the town for her economic support.[14]

Rather than turn to public charity, some estranged wives without kin and economic resources attempted to support themselves by working as servants in the households of other community members. When Uriah Hayes wrote in his notice that he "had rather see the delicacy of the Cheek and hand tarnished with labor to procure subsistence than any other way," he revealed his expectation that his eloped wife Rachel would turn to working as a servant, cook, or laundress to support herself. In Polly Montgomery's response to her husband Hugh's notice, in which he had claimed that "ever since her departure, [she had] in an unbecoming, scandalous, unlawful manner cohabited with other men," she defended herself by asserting that "I have hitherto by honest industry in a reputable family procured sustenance for myself and child." Until the 1820s, when newly constructed textile mills began to hire young women as factory hands, few employments other than household service or work as seamstresses existed for women seeking to support themselves in New England communities.[15]

Estranged wives who sought public relief or worked as servants remained dependent on and subordinate to town officials or their masters. These women might have preferred dependence on poor relief or another head of household to dependence on their husbands; however, some women who remained apart from their spouses sought out a more independent existence. While a few of these women achieved notable success, an examination of the strategies they pursued to support themselves demonstrates that they never truly escaped the limitations of their dependent legal status.

In November of 1798, Fanny Baker placed an advertisement in the *Vergennes Gazette*:

> This is to certify, That I Fanny Baker, now living in Vergennes, have for these two years past, without the help of my husband, Josiah Baker, received my subsistence and support through my own means, and having it in my power to continue providing for myself, I take this opportunity, through the medium of a public newspaper, of making known this my determination of doing as well as I can.

Baker's claim that she had supported herself successfully for two years suggests that economic opportunities for women did exist in early national New England communities. Yet, the fact that she had to print such a notice is evidence that Baker and her fellow community members had good reason to believe that she would not succeed. The notice does not state the specific problems with which Baker had to contend, but as a newcomer to Vergennes, and especially as a married woman living apart from her husband, she might have had trouble persuading shop owners to extend her credit or convincing other townspeople to do business with her. Her absent husband's legal right to her profits or produce threatened Baker's ability to conduct her own business successfully.[16]

Fanny Baker's notice was an attempt to claim economic independence in spite of her status as a married woman. Several scholars have noted examples of married women in the early republic conducting their own businesses without having obtained legal status as *femes sole*. In contrast to the *feme covert*, the *feme sole* had the right to buy and sell property, to enter into contracts, to sue and be sued in her own name. Such legal rights were crucial to the successful operation of any business enterprise. Linda Kerber notes that early national courts legitimized married women acting as *femes sole* if there was proof that the women's husbands approved of their business activities. However, when husbands deserted their wives, courts would not presume their consent to the women's actions in the market. It was necessary for these estranged wives to petition state legislatures for permission to conduct themselves as *femes sole*.[17] Although Baker did not reveal the nature of her business in her advertisement, it is clear that she was operating as a *feme sole* without proper legal recognition. Many women may have operated successfully under these circumstances; however, the 1826 case of *Robinson v. Reynolds* reveals the potential legal hazards of these women's situations.[18]

In this case, the Vermont Supreme Court rejected the appeal of Franklin Robinson, a merchant who had sued Elisha Reynolds for payment for goods Robinson had delivered to Reynolds's wife before the couple's marriage. The court decided against Robinson because at the time of the transaction, Sally Reynolds had been married to but living separately from another man. Robinson claimed that he had dealt with Sally as a *feme sole,* but the court rejected the notion that a married woman could act as an independent economic agent even if she had lived apart from her husband for many years. The court's decision affirmed Chancellor James Kent's warning that "all persons supplying the food, lodging, and raiment of a married woman living separate from her husband are bound to make inquiries, and they give credit at their peril." Cases such as *Robinson v. Reynolds* would have increased merchants' and artisans' reluctance to deal with married women living apart from their husbands, for they had no legal guarantee of payment for goods or services. The court's decision reinforced the fact that the law continued to recognize such women as dependents of their husbands. Regardless of their economic success, the law encumbered these women with all the disabilities of *femes covert.*[19]

Wives living apart from their husbands pursued various strategies to free themselves from their legal disabilities. An examination of the lives of Julia Thomas and Rachel Winslow reveals the varying levels of success such wives obtained, as well as the different degrees of dependence that defined these women's lives. Both Thomas and Winslow lived apart from their husbands without divorcing, and both managed to obtain adequate economic support. Each woman pursued a different path to achieve her goal; however, neither path led to true independence.

In 1807, Titus Thomas of Hartford, Connecticut, announced that his wife Julia had left him because of "my misbehavior to her." In spite of acknowledging that he was to blame for the couple's separation, Titus went on to deny Julia access to his credit. The couple did not reconcile; instead, they took steps to enable Julia to continue to live apart from Titus and to receive adequate economic support without relying on his credit. Earlier in their marriage, Julia and her three siblings had inherited a piece of property from their father. In the years following their separation, Titus and Julia took steps to clear this land from any claims. Land records reveal that Titus paid mortgages held against the property and purchased

the other siblings' shares of the property. When the property had been secured, Titus sold it to the town of Hartford, which would "hold & dispose of said granted premises for the support and benefit of my wife."
The sale of this property to the town enabled Julia Thomas to live separately from her husband, without fearing that he or his creditors would
take the property. However, Julia was far from independent; instead, she
remained dependent on the Hartford town officials who would manage
the property for her benefit. Because of legal prohibitions against the
transfer of property from husband to wife while the marriage endured,
Titus could not sell this property to Julia. Selling the property to the town
allowed Julia to receive economic support while living apart from her
husband; however, it also continued her dependent status. Julia Thomas
achieved her goal of remaining separated from her husband while remaining economically secure. The price of that economic security was her
continuing dependence.[20]

In March of 1821, Rachel White married Kenelm Winslow at Bridgewater, Vermont. The couple quickly grew disillusioned with one another,
for the following October Kenelm placed an advertisement in the Woodstock *Observer*: "Notice is hereby given, that the subscriber and his wife
Rachael [sic] have parted, and agreed to live separately hereafter. All persons are forbid trusting or keeping her on my account, as I shall pay no
debts of her contracting after this date." In the years following this advertisement, Rachel Winslow conducted herself as a *feme sole*, a single
woman with the right to own property, enter into contracts, and sue and
be sued. In 1820, before she married Kenelm, Rachel had purchased fourteen acres of land in Bridgewater for thirty dollars. Three months after
Kenelm announced their separation, Rachel sold this piece of land and
another thirty-acre lot for $250. She then bought twenty-four acres—half
of a farm—from Enoch White, who was probably her brother. In 1830,
the Bridgewater Grand List assessed taxes on Rachel's property, testifying
to her continued independent status.[21]

Rachel Winslow appears to have acted with a great deal more daily independence than Julia Thomas. Thomas remained dependent on the
town of Hartford to manage property for her, while Winslow actively
bought and sold property on her own, making independent judgments
and taking independent actions. However, a closer look at Rachel
Winslow's experience reveals the limitations her legal status as a married
woman placed on her daily independence. In his advertisement, Kenelm
Winslow stated that he and Rachel had agreed to separate. The couple no

longer wished to live together and Kenelm did not take any steps to prevent Rachel from living on her own. He allowed Rachel to reclaim the property she had brought into the marriage and use it to support herself. Kenelm Winslow could have prevented his wife from acting as an independent agent in the marketplace. Wives had no right by law to buy and sell anything in their own names. The law was not proactive, however; it did not prohibit married women from completing transactions in the marketplace. Unless a husband challenged these transactions, the law assumed his consent. Kenelm Winslow never challenged his wife's transactions because he did not wish to interfere with Rachel's attempts to support herself. Because Rachel had not deserted, Kenelm remained legally responsible for her economic support after the separation. If he wished to continue to live apart from his wife without supporting her, he had to allow her to act independently in the marketplace. The independent actions of Rachel Winslow were rooted in her husband's implicit approval.

Another factor in the Winslows' situation was their lack of financial difficulties. Only once did Kenelm Winslow appear in county court on any action relating to debt. On this occasion, a creditor sued him for $234. The court found in favor of the creditor, whom Winslow promptly paid. This relative lack of court appearances for debt suggests that Kenelm Winslow either went into debt infrequently or paid his debts promptly. The lack of claims against Winslow's estate contributed to Rachel's ability to support herself independently. By law, the land that Rachel purchased belonged to her husband and therefore was subject to the claims of her husband's creditors. Rachel's position as an independent economic agent depended on the absence of claims against Kenelm's estate. Unlike Julia Thomas, Rachel Winslow was not dependent on a third party to manage property for her benefit. However, she *was* dependent on her husband's willingness to allow her to act independently and on her husband's ability to stay out of debt.[22]

Kenelm and Rachel Winslow were one of twenty-one Vermont and Connecticut couples in this study who, between 1790 and 1830, publicly announced their mutual decisions to separate.[23] The historian Hendrik Hartog has argued persuasively that such announcements were not mere substitutes for divorce. Hartog maintains that most Americans were committed to the ideal of marriage as a life-long relationship. He argues that couples who posted mutual separation notices wanted to remain married; however, they wished to live separately. In order to do so, husbands and wives needed to ensure that the women had access to adequate economic support. In 1810, Thomas Brigham claimed that "I have given to my wife Polly Brigham, sufficient property for her separate maintenance." Likewise, Levi Ball announced that "Thankful, my wife, left my house in Oct. last, by agreement between her and myself—we then divided property and agreed to live separate during life, without assisting each other." These husbands believed that by giving their wives property, they were absolved from providing any further support for the women. Husbands such as Ebenezer Couch, who announced that "by mutual agreement she [his wife Hannah] is to provide for herself and I am to do as I can," intended their notices to persuade community members to deny their wives access to their credit *and* to allow the women to support themselves independently. As long as these men wished to remain free of their legal obligation to support their wives, they would refrain from interfering in the women's attempts to support themselves. These wives were free to act independently in the marketplace, but that freedom depended on their husbands' goodwill and on the *men's* continued desire to live separately.[24]

Their husbands' tacit consent formed the precarious foundation on which these women based their ability to support themselves. Married women who lived apart from their husbands were in a vulnerable position. These women could take advantage of opportunities to act in their own interests, but they could not ensure the continued existence of those opportunities. Women living apart from their husbands could cross the fine line between opportunity and limitation without warning. A husband's decision to claim what was legally his property or his financial difficulties could defeat a married woman's attempt to live independently. The case of Margaret Martin Gaylord demonstrates how a woman's own death could frustrate what had been a remarkable example of an economically independent married woman.

In the early 1770s, Margaret Martin and her husband James emigrated from Scotland to Springfield, Vermont, where they ran a tavern on the Crown Point Road connecting Boston with Montreal. The Martins had three children: twins James and Mary, who were born in 1775 but did not survive long, and a son, William, born in 1779. James Martin died on October 5, 1789. Two years later, on October 20, 1791, Margaret married Moses Gaylord. They continued to run the renamed Gaylord Tavern until March of 1795, when they separated. Moses announced their separation in the *Vermont Journal*: "Notice is hereby given, that Moses Gaylord, and his wife Margaret, have dissolved their connections, by their mutual consent." The couple never reconciled: Moses moved to New York while Margaret remained in Springfield. No record exists of a divorce.[25]

After the separation, Margaret prospered. Her name appears as the head of household on the 1800 and 1810 federal censuses. Margaret and her son, William, sold mineral rights on their farm in 1801. After William's death, Margaret leased out land in her own name in 1808. She appeared in Windsor County Court three times to defend herself against debt actions. Although she was successful only once, she quickly paid the judgments in the other two cases. She died on February 29, 1836, in possession of a 100–acre farm. Margaret had lived as an independent woman for forty years: local justices of the peace, judges of the county court, and even federal census takers had accepted her as a de facto head of household. However, after her death, Springfield town officials and the probate court thwarted Margaret Gaylord's attempt to devise what she believed was her property.[26]

In her will, she left "all the Real & personal Property of which I am possessed and have been for more than thirty years" to "my beloved friend William Goodenough, who now is and has been a resident with me for a number of years last past, and has been my friend in sickness and old age." Gaylord signed the will with a mark (as she had signed the deed and lease to which she had been party) and three witnesses also signed the document testifying that the will was Gaylord's true intent. The selectmen of Springfield immediately questioned the validity of the will and, at a town meeting on March 29, 1836, they asked the voters to decide if they should take any measures to obtain title to the farm. The selectmen based their request on an 1821 statute that allowed towns to petition the probate court to escheat an estate with no legal heirs and to assign the estate to the trustees of schools. However, Springfield citizens voted against authorizing the selectmen to take any measures to obtain the Gaylord estate.[27]

The townspeople's vote against challenging Gaylord's will suggests that community members accepted Gaylord's de facto independent status, and recognized her ability to devise property. However, town selectmen knew that Gaylord's de jure status as a married woman was grounds to overturn the will. In spite of the negative vote, the selectmen did challenge the will, and in August of 1836 the probate court declared "that said Instrument be . . . disallowed and disapproved." The wording of the court's decision is imprecise and indicates only that the court was not satisfied that the will had been properly sealed. Vermont law required that a will be sealed with the signature or mark of the testator and with the signatures of three witnesses. Since Margaret Gaylord's will met these requirements, it is difficult to know on what grounds the court based its decision. No doubt the court was concerned about the legal propriety of allowing a married woman to devise an estate to which her legal claim was unclear. The fact that Gaylord wished to grant the estate to her lover also added a moral dimension to the case that the court would have had difficulty ignoring.[28]

The court ordered that the estate be sold and that an announcement of Gaylord's death be placed in the newspapers to advise any legal heirs to appear before the court to present their claims to the estate. The only person who had any legal claim to Margaret Gaylord's property was her husband, Moses, who in all probability was no longer living. Had he responded to the court's announcement, Moses Gaylord would have been entitled to receive all of Margaret's personal property and any property she had acquired during their marriage. No heirs appeared to claim the Gaylord estate, and in March of 1838 the probate court assigned the $1,179 remaining after the sale and settlement of the estate to the trustees of Springfield's schools.[29]

Margaret Gaylord's life and death provide a telling example of both the opportunities available to and the limitations faced by married women in the early republic. Like other married women, Gaylord believed that she could act independently and that she could own and even devise property. However, in spite of Margaret Gaylord's successful attempt to live independently, upon her death, her legal disabilities as a *feme covert* closed in on her.

The lives of women who experienced marital conflict offer evidence of the very real pressures and limitations the law placed on married women. Husbands could compel their wives' return and obedience by denying them credit, and any woman living apart from her husband faced a precarious existence in a society that legally denied her the right to own property or her own wages. The law denied all married women—even those living apart from their husbands—the full measure of economic independence. Women could maneuver around the law in their daily lives, but only if their husbands agreed not to interfere. Regardless of their individual efforts and circumstances, these women remained dependent on their husbands. When his wife Anna eloped in June of 1814, Joseph Ayres declared that "having confidence in her own abilities, [she] has actually departed, with a view to live separately, contrary to the desire of the marriage institution, and greatly to my disadvantage." No matter how confident or capable Anna Ayres was, unless she could rely on kin or other economic resources, her husband could ensure that her attempt to live separately was to *her* great disadvantage. Anna Ayres recognized that opportunities for married women to support themselves did exist; however, her husband had the legal power to prevent Anna from realizing these opportunities. Joseph Ayres's notice indicates that he did not intend to allow Anna to succeed.[30]

The experiences of women who remained separated from their husbands reveal the contradictory nature of married women's status. The lives of estranged wives demonstrate that their dependent subordination was not absolute, but was fluid and negotiable. Married women living apart from their husbands sometimes were able to support themselves and act independently in the legal and economic arenas. However, their independence depended on their husbands' willingness to allow them to act as *femes sole*. The daily independence that these women experienced and their legal dependence on their husbands were intertwined. Estranged wives who supported themselves independently were able to moderate their subordinate status. However, they were able to do so only with their husbands' consent. Estranged wives remained *femes covert,* and if their husbands chose to interfere in their activities, these women remained subject to all the disabilities associated with coverture. Some women successfully coped with these contradictions; however, for others the tensions between independence and dependence were too great. These women sought a formal end to their dependent subordination and turned to the courts to end their marriages. These wives discovered that while divorce resolved some of the contradictions that entrapped estranged wives, it did not erase all of the limitations of dependent subordination.

6

"Free and Clear from All Claims"
Divorce and the Contradictory Nature of Women's Status

In January of 1818, Eunice Snow of Cavendish, Vermont, appeared before the Vermont Supreme Court to petition for divorce from her husband, Daniel. Snow claimed that on July 1, 1817, her husband's intolerable severity had driven her from his home. The court granted Snow a divorce but did not award her alimony. Slightly more than ten years later, in October of 1828, Eunice Snow died. She had accumulated a modest estate between the time of her divorce and the time of her death. According to probate records, her executor sold her personal property and 1.5 acres of land for $135, which Snow's will bequeathed to her two children. Although the records do not reveal how Snow acquired her property, it is clear that she retained close ties to her family of origin, members of which may have offered her important economic support. Two of the witnesses to Snow's will were her brother and sister-in-law, David and Melinda Whitcomb. Snow also appointed her "well beloved brother" Thomas Whitcomb as executor of her estate. The nature of the assistance Snow received from her siblings is unclear; however, it is likely that she lived with one of her brothers, as she does not appear independently on any census listing after the divorce, and the real estate she owned did not contain a house.[1]

For Eunice Snow, divorce resolved some of the contradictions related to her status as a married woman living apart from her husband. By legally removing her from her husband's authority, divorce enabled Snow to accumulate and devise property in her own name, free from any interference from her former husband. However, although a divorce decree legally freed Eunice Snow from dependence on her husband, she became dependent on kin for her support. Eunice Snow remained a dependent her entire life. As a daughter in her father's home, a wife in Daniel Snow's household, and a sister in her brother's home, Eunice legally was subordinate to male household heads. Yet, as a divorced woman living in her brother's home, Snow's dependent subordination did not deprive her of all opportunities to act in her own interest. Had Eunice remained married, she would not have had the opportunity to acquire an estate in her own name and to devise that estate to her children. In fact, in economic terms, Eunice appears to have fared better than her former husband. When Daniel Snow died in 1841, he left nothing to his children by his first marriage. Daniel owned no real estate, and the court-appointed administrator valued his personal estate at eighty-one dollars, which the court assigned to his second wife to support herself and the couple's minor children. Although Eunice Snow's divorce did not provide her with alimony and left her dependent on kin, legally ending her marriage freed Snow from an abusive husband and allowed her to pursue her own interests in ways that would not have been possible had she remained married.[2]

In the early national period, divorce did not free women completely from the contradictions that permeated their lives. Yet it did offer women greater opportunities to moderate their dependence and assert their own interests. Divorce freed women from abusive husbands and unhappy marriages. Divorce also granted women the legal rights to remarry and to conduct business in their own names. Divorced women were able to claim their own wages and own and devise property. In cases of desertion, divorce also allowed some women to escape responsibility for the debts of their absent husbands. For women who sought and obtained alimony, divorce provided a division of property that could help them support themselves. For most divorced women, however, the formal restoration of *feme sole* status did not erase completely the limitations of dependent subordination. Because most divorced women could not support themselves, divorce usually left women dependent on family members, friends, or second husbands. Divorce provided women with opportunities to which they would not have had access had they remained married, but it did not entirely remove the disabilities of dependent subordination.

Scholars who study divorce have offered contrasting assessments of the degree to which divorce did or did not benefit women in the postrevolutionary era. In an article on divorce in eighteenth-century Massachusetts, Nancy Cott interprets the rising frequency with which women sought divorce and their increasing rate of success in obtaining divorces as evidence of women's improved status within the family and of women's increased autonomy. However, scholars such as Glenda Riley, who praise more liberal divorce laws because they supported greater personal freedom and fulfillment, caution that inadequate and unenforceable alimony awards left divorced women in precarious situations. Historians who focus on the economic implications of divorce argue that even if women in the postrevolutionary period exercised a new-found sense of independence by suing for divorce, their inability to support themselves after obtaining divorce decrees left them mired in economic dependence. Linda Kerber claims that few Americans acknowledged that revolutionary rhetoric emphasizing independence and freedom from tyranny offered theoretical support for more lenient divorce laws. She asserts that "divorce in the Revolutionary era was not the mark of liberation: it was the gambit of the desperate." In a study of divorce in nineteenth-century New York and Indiana, Norma Basch argues that because most women who obtained divorces did not receive alimony, divorce left women unable to support themselves economically. She believes that the most important form of relief that divorce offered women was the right to remarry, a right that guaranteed their continued dependence on men.[3]

An examination of the lives of estranged New England wives who sought divorce reveals a complex picture of the reasons women turned to divorce and the benefits they received from it. Divorce did not necessarily provide women with greater independence; in fact, women in the early republic would not have identified independence as a realistic or desirable goal. However, neither did women divorce solely for the right to remarry. Very few women in the sample population remarried after divorcing: records reveal that only one Connecticut woman and two Vermont women remarried after they obtained divorces. In fact, evidence from Vermont, where twenty-two divorced men married again, suggests that men were far more likely than women to remarry after divorcing.[4] The desire to regain *feme sole* status so that they could retain access to property and wages appears to have been a more significant factor motivating New England women to seek divorce. Estranged wives were aware of the contradictions they faced as married women living apart from their husbands. These women remained subject to all the disabilities of coverture, even if they supported themselves without any assistance from their spouses. Because of their *feme covert* status, their husbands legally could claim the property and wages of estranged wives. If their husbands had deserted, the men's creditors could attach these women's wages and property to pay their absent spouses' debts. Those women who sought divorce hoped that legally ending their marriages would resolve these contradictions. Divorce restored women to *feme sole* status, a change that freed women from the disabilities of coverture by erasing their legal dependence on their husbands. However, in spite of this release from coverture, dependence continued to characterize divorced women's lives. New England women in the early national period did not seek or receive independence when they divorced; rather, divorce offered them a chance to moderate their dependence to allow them opportunities to assert their interests and shape their lives in ways that would not have been possible had they remained married.

Vermont and Connecticut women most frequently petitioned for divorce on the grounds of desertion (see tables 5 and 6). For wives who had been deserted, and for women whose husbands had abused them, the contradictions inherent in the common law marriage contract were especially striking. According to the common law, when they married, these women gave up their legal identities, their wages, and control over their property in exchange for their husbands' support and protection. Instead of finding that support and protection, these wives had been abandoned or abused. Yet, in spite of their husbands' flagrant violations of the marriage contract, these women remained subject to all the disabilities of coverture. Such wives pursued divorce to escape this contradiction.

For the women who claimed that their husbands had abused them, freedom from *feme covert* status and their husbands' authority often was a matter of survival. In 1819, Temperance Hill claimed that for ten years her husband Allen "repeatedly beat[,] bruted & most cruelly & without cause or provocation, treated your Petitioner that he frequently threatened the life of your Petitioner & treated her with such excessive cruelty that she was obliged in order to save her life, as she verily believes, to leave him." Anna Kittredge also complained that her husband's cruel be-

TABLE 5

Grounds on Which Vermont Women Petitioned for Divorce[a]

	Number	Percentage
Desertion	125	67
Intolerable Severity	89	48
Adultery	58	31

[a] Based on 186 petitions from Chittenden, Washington, and Windsor counties between 1790 and 1830. The table indicates the number and percentage of petitions that contained each complaint. Because petitions often contained more than one complaint, the total numbers exceed 186 and total percentages exceed 100 percent.

TABLE 6

Grounds on Which Connecticut Women Petitioned for Divorce[a]

	Number	Percentage
Desertion	172	69
Intolerable Severity	53	21
Adultery	55	22

[a] Based on 190 petitions to the Connecticut Superior Court while it sat at Hartford County between 1790 and 1830 and on fifty-eight petitions presented to the Connecticut Assembly between 1789 and 1818. The table indicates the number and percentage of petitions that contained each complaint. Because petitions often contained more than one complaint, the total numbers exceed 248 and total percentages exceed 100 percent.

havior and threats "hath put her in great fear," and in Abigail Bedient's 1801 petition, she accused her husband Gilead of attempting to take her life. The experiences of these women belied the promise of the traditional marriage covenant. Instead of receiving security and protection in exchange for their dependent subordination, these wives feared for their lives. Only by divorcing their husbands could abused women find the security that marriage had failed to provide.[5]

Women who petitioned for divorce on the grounds of desertion also hoped to escape the contradictions of *feme covert* status. These women frequently expressed economic concerns in their divorce petitions, often accusing their husbands of failing to provide economic support. Although it was not separate grounds for divorce, a husband's failure to provide for his wife supported her claim that he had neglected his marital obligations. In addition, according to the common law, the mere fact of a husband's physical absence was not sufficient evidence of his desertion. The law did not require that husbands reside with their wives; however, it did insist that husbands support their spouses. A husband could leave his wife indefinitely without being guilty of desertion as long as he continued to provide her with necessaries. In order to receive a divorce on the grounds of desertion, wives had to convince the court that their husbands had failed to fulfill the economic obligations of the marriage contract. Under these legal circumstances, it is not surprising that many New England wives who sued for divorce framed their petitions in an economic context.

However, legal requirements only partly explain why wives emphasized economic concerns in their divorce petitions. Marital conflict often resulted in real economic hardship for women. In her 1828 divorce petition, Sabrina Cooley explained that her husband's cruelty had forced her to leave his home and that she "had been obliged to rely for a meagre [sic] and precarious subsistence upon her own personal labour and the charity of her friends." When husbands deserted or their cruelty forced their wives to leave, the women often faced real deprivation. Unless a husband who deserted left property behind, his wife would have had great difficulty supporting herself. Even when a deserted wife had access to a significant amount of property, she still had to cope with the loss of an adult male worker. Without access to property, and in an era of limited employment opportunities, most estranged wives' economic opportunities were meager and precarious indeed.[6]

Women's petitions also reveal another cause for their economic concerns: the presence of children. In 1807, Anna Chamberlin claimed that her husband Asa "has gone to parts unknown to your petitioner and left her destitute of support for herself and Infant child." Likewise, when Jemima Sill petitioned for divorce in 1808, she revealed that she had "eight small children" to support.[7] When husbands deserted, the responsibility of providing for their children fell to their wives. Moreover, the evidence reveals that minor children were more likely to reside with their mothers after their parents had separated regardless of whether their fathers had deserted. Of a sample population of sixty-three Vermont couples who divorced between 1790 and 1830, at least forty-two had minor children living at the time of the divorce. The whereabouts of the children are unknown in 43 percent of these cases. However, in cases where court, census, and probate records reveal the status of the children, Vermont mothers retained sole custody 75 percent of the time. The evidence from Connecticut is not as complete, but it is suggestive. Of the 251 divorce petitions presented to the Connecticut Superior Court sitting in Hartford County between 1790 and 1830, twenty mentioned children that the petitioner was supporting. In all twenty cases, the petitioner was a woman. In addition, ten women who petitioned the Connecticut General Assembly for divorce also petitioned for the custody of their children. The assembly awarded these women custody every time it granted their divorce petitions. Not one man who petitioned the assembly for divorce requested custody of his children; instead, men were more likely to petition for divorce decrees so that they could *stop* supporting children they did not believe were their own.[8] For women, receiving custody of their children was a mixed blessing. Regardless of the personal satisfaction mothers received from raising their children, the responsibility of providing for sons and daughters tremendously increased the economic difficulties that divorced women faced.

Estranged wives' legal status complicated their economic troubles. Even if their husbands had left property behind or if these wives were able to work to support themselves, their wages and property legally belonged to their husbands. If their husbands had any outstanding debts, creditors could attach the property and the women's wages. After Isaac Hall had posted a notice denying her access to his credit, his wife Sarah asserted that she had supported him for two years and that he had left her. She also declared that "I wish none of his creditors to call on me for his debts." Regardless of her wishes, as long as she remained married to Isaac, his creditors legally could attach Sarah's property or wages to pay his debts. In 1811, Sarah petitioned for a divorce on the grounds of desertion, asking the court to grant her a decree "freeing her from all the obligations she was under to the said Isaac by law of the marriage covenant," obligations that included satisfying the demands of Isaac's creditors. When Harriot Allen divorced her husband Rufus in 1812, the court granted her alimony and decreed that

> the said Harriot shall hold and possess the said enumerated articles aforesaid, as of her own personal property . . . free and clear from all claims which the said Rufus Allen, or the creditors of the said Rufus, have or had, or might have or had, by reason of the Coverture occasioned by the intermarriage of the said Rufus and the said Harriot.

Only divorce protected the economic interests of women such as Harriot Allen and Sarah Hall from the interference of their spouses or the men's creditors.[9]

Other women also appear to have used divorce as a way to escape responsibility for their husbands' debts and to legitimate their possession of their husbands' property. On July 19, 1813, John and Abigail Rice of Hartland, Vermont, placed a notice in the *Vermont Journal* in which they announced that "the parties do hereby mutually agree to part with each other." The couple also agreed to divide property. Abigail and the couple's only daughter continued to live in a house on a half-acre plot that legally belonged to John Rice. This arrangement suited Abigail for almost four years; however, in January of 1817 she petitioned for divorce on the grounds of desertion. The court granted her the divorce and awarded her the house and plot of land as alimony. Shortly after the divorce, county court records and executions for judgments found in Hartland land records reveal that John Rice encountered financial problems and had difficulty paying his debts. Abigail Rice's decision to legally end her marriage coincided with her husband's looming financial troubles. By divorcing him and receiving legal title to her home, Abigail protected this property from her husband's creditors.[10]

Like Rice, Marcy Moor of Granby, Connecticut, used divorce as a means to secure support from her husband Amasa's financially troubled estate. The Moors' marital difficulties dated back to 1799, when Amasa advertised Marcy's elopement and denied her credit. In her 1807 divorce petition, Marcy claimed that Amasa had committed adultery and deserted in 1800. Marcy was quite knowledgeable about her husband's property: in her petition she provided details concerning the location and value of Amasa's real estate. The Connecticut Superior Court awarded her a divorce and a portion of Amasa's real property, worth approximately one-third of his one-thousand-dollar estate. Hartford County Court records from this time period reveal that Amasa Moor's hold on his estate was precarious, at best. Amasa was operating under the supervision of a town-appointed overseer, a method that towns resorted to when it appeared that a resident was not capable of managing his own affairs in a competent manner. Amasa's overseer was involved in settling debts against the estate, the size and value of which were diminishing as a result of debt suits and various land transactions. By divorcing her husband before his mismanagement reduced his estate even further, Marcy Moor shrewdly secured her own economic support.[11]

Protecting property of which they had de facto possession was an important motivating factor for women seeking divorce. Married women who possessed property as a result of their husbands' desertion or informal separation agreements directly confronted the ambiguities of *feme covert* status. The law did not prevent these women from managing their husbands' estates or businesses, but they did so knowing that their husbands or their husbands' creditors could claim legal ownership of this property. In a sermon denouncing divorce because of the harm he believed it brought to women, Yale College president Timothy Dwight argued,

> *The divorced wife is more injured than the deserted wife.* . . . She is forced by violence from her husband, her children, and her home. She is turned out with disgrace; as a woman, with whom her husband could not continue to live; and usually with little provision made for her subsistence. The wife, who is deserted, is on the contrary, almost always left

in the possession of her house, her children, her character, and tolerable means of subsistence for herself and her family.

What Dwight failed to recognize, but what every deserted woman knew, was that these wives' possession of their homes and means of subsistence was legally tenuous and subject to the interference of their husbands and their husbands' creditors. Only divorce aligned estranged wives' legal status with their de facto possession and management of property.[12]

The experience of Mary Watkins demonstrates that marital separation was not always a factor in provoking a wife to take action to obtain legal ownership of property that she had managed for years. Mary Scarborough had married John Watkins in 1777 at Ashford, Connecticut. The couple was living in Pomfret, Vermont, by 1778, when the first of their eight children was born. John purchased a 98–acre farm in Pomfret, and the family prospered for many years. However, in 1801, several freeholders petitioned the Pomfret selectmen "to make inquiry whether John Watkins of said Pomfret be *non compos mentis.*" After an investigation, the selectmen determined that Watkins was not of sound mind and appointed a guardian to watch over the family's economic affairs. It is impossible to determine how active the guardian was in managing the Watkins' affairs; however, Mary Watkins would have been responsible for many of the day-to-day decisions regarding the farm's operation. The Watkins family remained under legal guardianship until August of 1811, when Mary sued for divorce on the grounds of intolerable severity. The court granted her petition and her request for alimony, awarding her sixty-eight acres of the farm, some cattle, and two-thirds of the household furniture and utensils to support herself and the four children who continued to live with her.[13]

Although she and her husband had not separated, Mary Watkins encountered the same contradiction between legal status and actual experience that estranged wives faced. John Watkins's mental incapacity left Mary to act as a de facto head of household. However, as a *feme covert,* Mary legally was subordinate to her husband's guardian. The guardian may have allowed Mary to manage the farm as she wished, but he legally had the power to make decisions regarding family affairs and to compel her obedience. Only divorce removed Mary from both her husband's abuse and the guardian's legal authority. Divorce and the accompanying alimony award eliminated the contradictions between Mary's legal subordination and a daily reality in which she managed a farm and provided for her family.

John Watkins died less than two years after the divorce. Because of his status as *non compos mentis,* the probate court administered his estate as if he had died intestate. The court strictly adhered to Vermont intestacy laws and divided the $459–estate among his children, with the sons receiving portions double those awarded to their sisters. Had Mary Watkins remained married to John, upon his death she would have received outright ownership of one-third of his personal property and the use rights to one-third of his real estate. Instead, because she had divorced John, at the time of his death Mary legally possessed more than two-thirds of John's original estate, both real and personal. Mary's divorce placed her in a far superior economic position than she would have been in as John Watkins's widow. Divorce not only offered Mary a way out of an intolerable marriage; it also provided her with greater economic security than she would have received had she remained married.[14]

Mary Watkins obtained a greater proportion of her husband's estate than did most other women who received alimony awards. Sixty-five percent of the Vermont wives who petitioned for alimony received an award; however, these women represent only 28 percent of *all* female divorce petitioners. As discussed in chapter 3, Connecticut Superior Court divorce decrees rarely mention alimony, although scattered evidence suggests that the court did award alimony more often than extant records indicate. The rate of alimony awards that the Connecticut General Assembly granted are roughly comparable to those of the Vermont Supreme Court: 55 percent of Connecticut women who petitioned the legislature for alimony received an award, a number that represents only 21 percent of *all* women petitioning the assembly for divorce. Although divorce removed many of the disabilities of women's subordination, the fact that the majority of women did not receive alimony meant that divorced women usually remained dependent on family, friends, or second husbands for support. In fact, even those women who received alimony frequently could not support themselves. Divorce changed women's legal status, but it did not alter a reality in which most women had limited access to property and other economic resources.

Because of the nature of the property awarded and because of the courts' and legislature's inability to enforce husbands' compliance, alimony frequently did not provide women with the opportunity to support themselves. Husbands' refusal to comply with alimony awards was especially problematic with cash grants. Cash awards were the most common type of alimony that Connecticut women received and the second most common type of alimony granted in Vermont.[15] In both Vermont and Connecticut, cash awards were fairly generous (see tables 7 and 8); however, unlike landed or personal property, which the court could order a constable to seize, women received cash awards only when their husbands were willing and able to comply with the alimony decree. In at least two cases in which the Vermont court awarded divorced women substantial cash settlements, the records reveal that the husbands avoided paying the money to their former wives. Neither Almena Hall, to whom the court granted a $750–cash award, nor Rachel Hayes, whose divorce decree included an order that her husband pay her $150 a year for the remainder of her life, received their cash awards. Cash grants left divorced women dependent on their husbands' willingness and ability to obey the decrees. No matter how generous the awards, cash grants did not guarantee women adequate economic support.[16]

Even when the courts and legislature were able to ensure that women received their alimony awards, the type of property included in the awards usually did not afford women adequate economic support. The most common type of property the Vermont court awarded to divorced women was household furniture and utensils. Seventy-two percent of all Vermont alimony awards included household items, and one-third of all awards consisted of *only* household goods. The value of these awards varied greatly. In 1813, the court granted Betsey Rice of Windsor, Vermont, household furnishings and utensils valued at fifty-seven dollars. In contrast, the list of household goods that the court granted Marcia Belden was almost a page long and included items such as fifteen chairs, a 130–piece china set, and a silver tea set and candlesticks. The alimony award that Harriot Allen received was fairly typical: the court granted Allen

TABLE 7
Size of Cash Awards, Vermont Supreme Court[a]

	Number	Percentage
Under $99	2	11
$100–$499	6	33
$500–$999	7	39
$1,000+	3	17

[a] Based on eighteen cash awards. The court awarded cash grants in twenty-two cases; however, the amount of the award was illegible in four cases.

TABLE 8
Size of Cash Awards, Connecticut Assembly[a]

	Number	Percentage
Under $99	0	0
$100–$499	3	43
$500–$999	1	14
$1000+	3	43

[a] Based on seven cash awards. The assembly awarded cash grants nine times; however, in two cases it did not specify the exact amount of the award.

"her wearing apparrel [sic] & ornaments; one set of China ware; one set of Crockery ware; one dining set; 3 beds with bedsteads, bedding & bed clothes; 3 looking glasses; one set silver tsps; one bureau; 3 tables; all kitchen utensils." Such awards generally did not provide women with the resources necessary to support themselves. Instead, awards of household furniture and utensils provided women with the tools to perform their traditional female labors in other men's households.[17]

Grants of household items allowed divorced women to become productive members in the households of new husbands or kinsmen. When Deborah Scott divorced her husband John in 1825, she received household furniture, linens, and wearing apparel as alimony. Within days of receiving her divorce, on June 19, 1825, Deborah married George Wilken. Her alimony award was not enough to support Deborah economically, but it allowed her to make an important economic contribution to her new husband's household. Alimony grants such as Deborah Scott's did not provide women with the means to live independently; rather, these awards reinforced the notion that women should perform their traditional labors within male-headed households.[18]

The most substantial alimony awards—those that did offer women a chance to support themselves independently—included land. However, 70 percent of Vermont awards and 65 percent of Connecticut alimony grants did *not* include real estate. Twenty-one Connecticut and Vermont women received land grants, with amounts ranging from the half-acre awarded to Abigail Rice (which she later sold for fifty dollars) to the 137–acre farm restored to Elizabeth Tilden (she had purchased the farm before her marriage).[19] Regardless of the size of these awards, Vermont and Connecticut jurists and legislators did not intend these land grants to support women's independence. In five of the twenty-one cases in which the courts and Connecticut legislature granted land as alimony, the women received land that they had inherited or purchased before marrying. In at least nine—and possibly fourteen—cases, the court awarded land to women for the primary purpose of supporting the couple's children.[20] Although such awards might be large enough to enable women to support themselves and their children independently, the court's *intent* in making these awards was to ensure the children's well-being, *not* the women's independence. As in the alimony decree of Polly Dustin, to whom the Vermont court granted twenty-five acres of land, the justices often removed full control of the property from the woman by ordering that the real estate "decend [sic] to the Children of said Polly by said Stephen [her former husband]." The Vermont court deprived women such as Polly Dustin of the right to devise the land they received as alimony and ensured that real property would pass to the lawful heirs of divorced men. Similarly, the wording of Connecticut Assembly decrees awarding land to divorced women clearly indicated that the assembly did not intend these women to have complete control over the property. In fact, the assembly never "gave" any woman property. Instead, when they granted Abigail Bedient a divorce, legislators passed a resolution "entitling her to occupy" one-third of her former husband's real estate. Connecticut legislators also passed resolutions granting women "the use of real estate" belonging to their former husbands, but they only intended such land awards to remain in effect while the women lived. After their deaths, the property in question returned to their former husbands' estates. The limited nature of such awards highlights the fact that economic support for the children— not economic independence for the woman—was New England jurists' and legislators' foremost goal.[21]

The insufficiency of most alimony awards made it difficult for divorced women to support themselves. Reliance on kin was a common strategy for women to follow after receiving a divorce. Living with kin ensured women's dependent status; however, many women may have preferred the subordination required of a daughter or sister to that required of a wife. Dependence on kin did not limit women's legal and economic options to the extent that marriage did. Like Eunice Snow, women who lived with family members could accumulate and devise property, actions that the law of coverture denied to wives. Likewise, living with kin did not prevent divorced women from conducting business in their own names. When Lois Hubbard divorced her husband Watts in 1811, she received as alimony her clothing, half of the household furniture, and $750 in notes due to her former husband. After her divorce, Lois did not support herself independently, but lived with her son Phineas and his family. Although she relied on her son, Lois Hubbard conducted her own business. When she died in 1838, her estate consisted of notes due and mortgages valued at $1,370. Dependence on her son did not prevent Hubbard from nearly doubling the worth of her alimony award. Divorce left Lois Hubbard dependent on kin; however, it also allowed her to conduct business in her own name, an opportunity that marriage denied her.[22]

Estranged wives faced many difficulties as they attempted to find ways to survive without their husbands' assistance. Most wives living apart from their husbands did not have access to significant amounts of property, and employment opportunities for women in early national New England were scarce. Married women's legal status compounded these difficulties by leaving them vulnerable to interference from their husbands and their husbands' creditors. Estranged wives often found themselves in the contradictory position of having to act independently in a society that legally denied them the right to do so. Some wives were able to live with this contradiction, but only if their husbands agreed not to interfere in their activities and if the men stayed out of debt. An abusive husband or one who was unable to pay his debts could make it impossible for an estranged wife to pursue her own interests. Divorce provided the only legal remedy to eliminate many of the contradictions inherent in estranged wives' status. By allowing women to act in the economic and legal arenas without interference, divorce opened opportunities for women that marriage had closed. Although most divorced women remained economically dependent, divorce offered women tangible legal benefits and allowed them to pursue their interests in ways that marriage had precluded. By divorcing their husbands, these women shaped the terms of their dependent subordination to allow themselves greater opportunities for self-assertion. Divorced women did not escape their subordinate status, but they did escape many of the contradictions they had faced as estranged wives. Divorce did not guarantee women freedom from dependence, but it offered them the chance to restructure that dependence to obtain security and perhaps a measure of personal happiness.

Afterword
Settling "All Matters of Dispute": Marital Conflict, Negotiation, and Compromise

On December 22, 1800, Stephen Hiscock of Union, Connecticut, posted an elopement notice in which he explained that his wife Thankful "has for several years past behaved herself towards me in a very unbecoming manner, and utterly refuses to do her duty towards me but has made it her practice to usurp my authority." Had married women's dependent subordinate status been as absolute as the doctrine of marital unity prescribed, Stephen and Thankful Hiscock's difficulties would not have led to Thankful's usurpation of her husband's authority, but to her submission to Stephen's will. However, in reality married women's dependent subordination was neither fixed nor absolute. Married couples had to negotiate the terms of wives' subordination, a process that elopement notices reveal was fraught with difficulty for many husbands and wives.[1]

In the early national period, daily reality and changing marital ideals presented couples with conflicts that the law could not easily resolve. Would a husband exercise his authority benevolently, or would he resort to physical coercion? Would a husband demand complete obedience, or would he solicit his wife's advice when making decisions? In addition, New England couples had to cope with the ways in which the early republic's changing economic and cultural terrain affected the marriage relationship. The transition to market capitalism highlighted the importance of women's household labors and created new opportunities for conflict between husbands and wives. Would men claim ownership and control of their wives' labors, or would women play a role in determining whether the products of their labors were used for household consumption, for exchange, or for sale? If their produce was sold or exchanged, would wives help determine the terms of exchange and would women participate in deciding how goods obtained in the market were used and distributed among family members? These points of potential conflict were especially acute in the late eighteenth and early nineteenth centuries, when cultural ideologies increasingly insisted on male economic independence and female domesticity.

The dictates of the law shaped the ways in which couples resolved these issues and the law granted husbands disproportionate power in setting the terms of their marriage relationships. Husbands could deny their wives access to their credit and they could insist on their spouses' obedience. Men could refuse to grant their wives any decision-making power and could limit their wives' access to the marketplace. However, in reality men needed their wives to act in the market and to make independent decisions to ensure their families' well-being. Most husbands recognized that the demands of daily existence made women's complete subordination impractical and undesirable. Wives also understood that their economic activities—as consumers, producers, and their husbands' agents—were indispensable to family survival. Women were convinced of the importance of their labors to their families' welfare, and they defended their rights and their opportunities to act in their own interests by pointing to their contributions to the household economy. However, married women also recognized that law and custom expected them to behave as obedient, faithful wives. For women in the early republic, marriage was a delicate balancing act between submission and dependence on the one hand, and self-assertion and partnership on the other.

The words and experiences of couples who experienced marital conflict reveal the difficulties inherent in assessing married women's status in the early national period. The legal doctrine of marital unity obscured the ambiguities of the law of coverture as well as the variations and contradictions of daily existence. The law established the parameters within which men and women constructed their marriage relationships, but these legal boundaries left considerable room for negotiation. On October 28, 1809, Benjamin Norris printed an advertisement in which he denied his wife, Lucy, credit after accusing her of eloping, stealing his property, and running him into debt. Several weeks later he printed another notice declaring,

> Whereas Lucy my wife and I have had a great deal of hardness towards each other, but have this day settled all matters of dispute between us. —

I have been so foolish as to give way to my passions so much that I feel willing to confess that I have treated my wife too hard in some cases. — I do feel happy in receiving her again.

Benjamin Norris was aware of the power that the law gave him over his wife and he did not hesitate to use that power to deprive her of access to his credit. However, Norris also was willing to settle "all matters of dispute" between him and Lucy, a willingness that led him to admit publicly that he had treated his wife "too hard in some cases." Benjamin and Lucy Norris understood that negotiation and compromise were necessary ingredients in a successful marriage. The law set the terms within which negotiation and compromise took place, and although the law privileged husbands and prescribed wives' subordination, Lucy Norris's success in obtaining a public admission of her husband's wrongdoing demonstrates that married women could maneuver within the confines of the law to create relationships that allowed them to assert their interests and defend their rights.[2]

Elopement notices appearing in New England newspapers reveal the issues over which married couples disagreed, as well as the strategies husbands and wives pursued to obtain satisfactory resolutions to their marriage conflicts in an era of exceptional cultural and economic change. These changes also affected the ways in which husbands and wives presented their marital conflicts to the public, as subtle shifts in couples' use of the notices by 1830 reveal. In both Connecticut and Vermont, the percentage of men who included details of their difficulties in their notices declined dramatically over this time period (see table 9). Husbands' advertisements became increasingly formulaic, and by the 1820s, the vast majority of men's notices consisted of little more than an accusation of desertion and a statement denying their wives credit. For their part, by the 1820s, New England wives increasingly chose not to respond to their husbands' notices (see table 10). These drops in the numbers of detailed notices and wives' postings suggest a growing reluctance to divulge the de-

TABLE 9

Percentage of Husbands Who Included Details in Their Notices

	No. of Notices	No. of Detailed Notices	% of Detailed Notices
1790–1799	286	154	54
1800–1809	388	186	48
1810–1819	479	189	40
1820–1829	429	128	30

TABLE 10
Percentage of Women Who Posted Notices

	No. of Men's Notices	No. of Women's Notices	% of Women's Notices
1790–1799	286	17	6
1800–1809	388	21	5.4
1810–1819	479	17	3.5
1820–1829	429	11	2.5

tails of marriage conflicts to the larger community. Desertion postings did not vanish; indeed, such advertisements continued to appear in newspapers even in the late twentieth century. However, given the absence of details in husbands' notices and the increased likelihood that wives would not report their versions of their conflicts, the meaning of these notices and the uses to which they were put shifted.

At the beginning of the period studied, husbands' and wives' notices served multiple purposes. Husbands intended their notices to deprive their wives of access to their credit, and wives fashioned their responses to negate the effects of their husbands' advertisements. Husbands and wives often included details of their spouses' bad behavior to gain support from community members, who could pressure husbands and wives to change their ways or offer shelter to runaway wives. Elopement notices sometimes served as announcements of permanent separation; at other times they were part of a process that resulted in reconciliation.

The occasional appearance of wives' postings served to remind readers that husbands' notices presented only one contested version of events. By the 1820s, however, notices increasingly served only one purpose: to announce a husband's refusal to pay his wife's debts. The lack of details in the notices and the greater infrequency of wives' postings helped to obscure the contested nature of husbands' accusations, lending men's versions of events a greater legitimacy. Couples continued to argue and negotiate, and they no doubt continued to rely on the support of neighbors, friends, and kin when marriages turned sour. However, estranged couples were less and less likely to appeal to the broader community for support.

Husbands' increased reluctance to reveal the details of their marital disputes and wives' decreased willingness to address the public through the newspapers indicate a growing preference for confining marriage to the private sphere. Scholars have identified the first third of the nineteenth century as a time when traditional patterns of community involvement in marriages existed alongside newer notions of domestic privacy, notions that would come to dominate nineteenth-century characterizations of family life. The "private" family was itself the product of other cultural and economic changes occurring in the early national period. The increased importance of love and affection in marriage and other family relationships, as well as the heightened significance of female domesticity and male wage earning contributed to growing distinctions between the public world of work and politics and the private world of home and family. Daily reality for many (if not most) Americans did not conform to this dichotomy between private and public; however, the ideal of the private domestic sphere acquired significant cultural power in the early national period.[3] The increasing importance of this ideal of family privacy is evident in elopement notices from the late eighteenth and early nineteenth centuries. While some couples openly solicited community involvement in their marital difficulties, increasing numbers of men and women agreed with John Woodruff, who wrote in his elopement notice that it was "distressing, mortifying . . . unfortunate for me to come forward in this way." Publicly revealing his dispute with his wife embarrassed Woodruff, but not enough to prevent him from publishing the notice. Such husbands were uncomfortable revealing the details of their marital conflicts to the public; however, they still did not hesitate to use their power to deny credit to their estranged wives. Ideals of domestic privacy did not diminish husbands' legal position as heads of households. Instead, because women's versions of events appeared less frequently, these ideals enhanced men's public displays of power over their wives. Husbands may have stopped including details in their advertisements in part because they felt that they no longer needed to justify to the larger community their "private" decisions to deprive their wives of their credit.[4]

Conflict between husbands and wives did not disappear completely from New England newspapers; however, the larger community increasingly read only sanitized statements declaring that conflict had occurred. Those who stood outside the inner circle of family, friends, and close neighbors were not privy to information regarding the causes of marriage conflicts or to wives' versions of events. The growing preference for shielding the details of marital difficulties from the larger community also obscured from the readers of New England's newspapers the ambiguous, contested nature of the law governing the marriage relationship. Marital conflict continued to occur, but husbands and wives increasingly negotiated between dependence and partnership, submission and self-assertion, behind closed doors, hidden from the larger community and historians alike.

Notes

ABBREVIATIONS OF WORKS CITED

BHL   Bailey Howe Library, University of Vermont, Burlington, Vt.

CALD   Connecticut Archives Lotteries and Divorces, Series 2, 1789–1820, Connecticut State Library, Hartford, Conn., microfilm.

CSL   Connecticut State Library, Hartford, Conn.

GSCSV General Services Center of the State of Vermont, Middlesex, Vt.

HCDR   Hartford County Divorce Records, 1740–1849, Connecticut State Library, Hartford, Conn., microfilm.

NEHGS New England Historic Genealogical Society, Boston, Mass.

VHS   Vermont Historical Society, Montpelier, Vt.

VRSV   Vital Records of the State of Vermont, 1760–1870, General Services Center of the State of Vermont, Middlesex, Vt., microfilm.

VSCR   Vermont Supreme Court Records, Vermont State Library, Montpelier, Vt., microfilm.

VSL   Vermont State Library, Montpelier, Vt.

WCCR   Windsor County Court Records, 1789–1825, Bailey Howe Library, University of Vermont, Burlington, Vt., microfilm.

WDPCR Windsor District Probate Court Records, General Services Center of the State of Vermont, Middlesex, Vt., microfilm.

NOTES TO THE INTRODUCTION

1. I have collected 1,187 elopement notices published between 1790 and 1830 in sixty-two extant Vermont newspapers, and 461 notices published during the same period in eight Hartford County, Connecticut, newspapers. In addition, a survey of the Northampton, Massachusetts, *Hampshire Gazette* revealed 117 notices published between 1790 and 1830, and a survey of the Portsmouth, New Hampshire, *Gazette* revealed seventy-nine desertion notices between 1790 and 1820, indicating that the number of notices found in Vermont and Connecticut newspapers was typical for newspapers throughout New England.

2. Levi Priest, *Reporter* [Brattleboro, Vt.], 1 March 1806.

3. William Blackstone, *Commentaries on the Laws of England*, 2 vols. (1765–1769, rpt. New York, 1836), 1:355–59. For an excellent discussion of the legal implications of *feme covert* status, see Linda K. Kerber, *Women of the Republic: Intellect and Ideology in Revolutionary America* (Chapel Hill: University of North Carolina Press, 1980), 139–55.

4. Blackstone, *Commentaries,* 1:355–59; James Kent, *Commentaries on American Law,* 4 vols. (1826, rpt. Boston, 1884), 2:185. For several examples of husbands' advertisements appearing under the heading of "Stray Wives," see Seth Moses's and Ebenezer Hooper's notices in the *Rutland* [Vt.] *Herald,* 9 September 1799, and Benjamin Stevens's notice in the *Vermont Mercury* [Rutland, Vt.], 11 April 1803.

5. On women's right to leave husbands who had treated them cruelly, see Kent, *Commentaries,* 2:157; and Tapping Reeve, *The Law of Baron and Feme, of Parent and Child, Guardian and Ward, Master and Servant, and of the Powers of the Courts of Chancery* (1816, rpt. Albany, N.Y., 1862), 160.

6. Betty Bandel, "What the Good Laws of Man Hath Put Asunder . . . ," *Vermont History* 46, no. 4 (1978): 221–33, an analysis of early national Vermont's lenient divorce laws, references elopement notices for what they reveal about women's perceptions of their marriages. Herman Lantz counted elopement notices in colonial newspapers as one indicator of marital conflict in "Marital Incompatibility and Social Change in Early America," *Sage Research Papers in the Social Sciences,* no. 4, Series Number: 90-026 (Studies of Marriage and the Family, 1976); Merril D. Smith, *Breaking the Bonds: Marital Discord in Pennsylvania, 1730–1830* (New York: New York University Press, 1991), 118, 139–40, mentions elopement notices as evidence of wives' desertions and briefly analyzes the content of several notices for what they reveal about sources of marital dissatisfaction. Jan Kurth, "Wayward Wenches and Wives: Runaway Women in the Hudson Valley, N.Y., 1785–1835," *NWSA Journal* (Winter 1988–1989): 199–220, focuses on elopement notices. However, Kurth does not analyze either the notices or the experience of marital separation. Her work is primarily descriptive.

7. Some of the best works that analyze married women's legal status are Norma Basch, *In the Eyes of the Law: Women, Marriage, and Property in Nineteenth-Century New York* (Ithaca, N.Y.: Cornell University Press, 1982); Norma Basch, *Framing American Divorce: From the Revolutionary Generation to the Victorians* (Berkeley: University of California Press, 1999); Nancy F. Cott, "Divorce and the Changing Status of Women in Eighteenth-Century Massachusetts," *William and Mary Quarterly,* 3rd series, 33, no. 4 (October 1976): 586–614; Nancy F. Cott, *Public Vows: A History of Marriage and the Nation* (Cambridge: Harvard University Press, 2000); Michael Grossberg, *Governing the Hearth: Law and the Family in Nineteenth-Century America* (Chapel Hill: University of North Carolina Press, 1985); Hendrik Hartog, *Man and Wife in Amer-*

ica: A History (Cambridge: Harvard University Press, 2000); Joan Hoff, *Law, Gender, and Injustice: A Legal History of U.S. Women* (New York: New York University Press, 1991); Kerber, *Women of the Republic*; Linda K. Kerber, *No Constitutional Right to Be Ladies: Women and the Obligations of Citizenship* (New York: Hill and Wang, 1998); Glenda Riley, *Divorce: An American Tradition* (New York: Oxford University Press, 1991); and Marylynn Salmon, *Women and the Law of Property in Early America* (Chapel Hill, N.C.: Institute for the Study of Early American History and Culture, 1986).

8. These works include Jeanne Boydston, *Home and Work: Housework, Wages, and the Ideology of Labor in the Early Republic* (New York: Oxford University Press, 1990); Nancy F. Cott, *The Bonds of Womanhood: "Woman's Sphere" in New England, 1780–1835* (New Haven, Conn.: Yale University Press, 1977); Carl N. Degler, *At Odds: Women and the Family in America from the Revolution to the Present* (New York: Oxford University Press, 1980); Anya Jabour, *Marriage in the Early Republic: Elizabeth and William Wirt and the Companionate Ideal* (Baltimore: Johns Hopkins University Press, 1998); Joan M. Jensen, *Loosening the Bonds: Mid-Atlantic Farm Women, 1750–1850* (New Haven, Conn.: Yale University Press, 1986); Catherine E. Kelly, *In the New England Fashion: Reshaping Women's Lives in the Nineteenth Century* (Ithaca, N.Y.: Cornell University Press, 1999); Suzanne Lebsock, *The Free Women of Petersburg: Status and Culture in a Southern Town, 1784–1860* (New York: Norton, 1984); Jan Lewis, *The Pursuit of Happiness: Family and Values in Jefferson's Virginia* (Cambridge: Cambridge University Press, 1983); Karen Lystra, *Searching the Heart: Women, Men, and Romantic Love in Nineteenth-Century America* (New York: Oxford University Press, 1989); Steven Mintz and Susan Kellogg, *Domestic Revolutions: A Social History of American Family Life* (New York: Free Press, 1988); Ellen K. Rothman, *Hands and Hearts: A History of Courtship in America* (Cambridge: Harvard University Press, 1987); Laurel Thatcher Ulrich, *Good Wives: Image and Reality in the Lives of Women in Northern New England, 1650–1750* (New York: Vintage Books, 1980); and Laurel Thatcher Ulrich, *A Midwife's Tale: The Life of Martha Ballard, Based on Her Diary, 1785–1812* (New York: Vintage Books, 1990).

9. For example, Cott, in *Bonds of Womanhood,* and Carroll Smith-Rosenberg, "The Female World of Love and Ritual: Relations between Women in Nineteenth-Century America," *Signs* 1, no. 1 (1975): 1–30, while not dismissing women's subordinate position within the household and in the larger society, draw attention to the positive attributes of "woman's sphere." On the other hand, Barbara Welter's foundational essay, "The Cult of True Womanhood, 1820–1860," *American Quarterly* 18, no. 2 (1966): 151–74, offers a more pessimistic assessment of the effects of the ideology of separate spheres on women. Boydston, *Home and Work,* argues that women's housework was devalued in the early national period, while Nancy Grey Osterud, *Bonds of Community: The*

Lives of Farm Women in Nineteenth-Century New York (Ithaca, N.Y.: Cornell University Press, 1991), maintains that while such devaluation occurred among the urban middle class, rural farm women's labors enabled them to modify gender relations in "a more symmetrical and egalitarian direction" (2).

10. Carole Shammas sees this body of mid-nineteenth-century legislation limiting patriarchal authority within the home as a manifestation of "the household's civil war," in *A History of Household Government in America* (Charlottesville: University of Virginia Press, 2002). Scholars who argue that married women in the early nineteenth century exercised greater autonomy in terms of control over property include Lebsock, *The Free Women of Petersburg,* and Salmon, *Women and the Law of Property.* In contrast, Hoff, *Law, Gender, and Injustice,* claims that greater limitations on dower rights, and increasing numbers of dower renunciations in the early national period "amount[ed] to a serious loss of economic holdings and economic influence of wives" (108). Again, such widely differing assessments of women's status are in keeping with the transitional nature of the period being studied.

11. Hartog, *Man and Wife,* esp. 93–135.

12. I am indebted to Kirsten Sword for alerting me to the uncertain legal standing of these newspaper postings. Sword does an excellent job of tracing the legal roots of the practice of posting elopement notices in her dissertation, "Wayward Wives, Runaway Slaves and the Limits of Patriarchal Authority in Early America" (Ph.D. diss., Harvard University, 2002), 47–67. For examples of popular legal handbooks' treatment of elopement notices, see [Giles Jacob], *Everyman His Own Lawyer* (New York, 1768), 212; [John M'Dougal], *The Farmer's Assistant; or, Every Man His Own Lawyer* (Chillicothe, Oh., 1813), 142.

13. U.S. Second Census, Connecticut, 1800. On the early history of Hartford and other Connecticut towns, see Bruce C. Daniels, *The Connecticut Town: Growth and Development, 1635–1790* (Middletown, Conn.: Wesleyan University Press, 1979) and Richard L. Bushman, *From Puritan to Yankee: Character and the Social Order in Connecticut, 1690–1765* (Cambridge: Harvard University Press, 1967).

14. U.S. Census, Vermont, 1800, 1810, 1820, 1830. On the development and growth of Windsor County, Vermont, towns, see Randolph A. Roth, *The Democratic Dilemma: Religion, Reform and the Social Order in the Connecticut River Valley of Vermont, 1791–1850* (Cambridge: Cambridge University Press, 1987) and William J. Gilmore, *Reading Becomes a Necessity of Life: Material and Cultural Life in Rural New England, 1780–1835* (Knoxville: University of Tennessee Press, 1989).

15. The Connecticut divorce statute is quoted in Kerber, *Women of the Republic,* 161. For the Vermont statute, see William Slade, Jr., ed., *Vermont State Papers* (Middlebury, 1823), 264; *Statutes of the State of Vermont* (Bennington, 1791), 50; William Slade, Jr., ed., *The Laws of Vermont, of a Publick and Per-*

manent Nature: Coming Down to and including the Year 1824 (Windsor, 1825), 363. See chapters 1 and 6 for an in-depth discussion of Vermont's and Connecticut's divorce laws.

16. VSCR, Windsor County, February 1794–June 1825, VSL, microfilm; HCDR, 1740–1849, CSL, microfilm; Barbara B. Ferris and Grace Louise Knox, eds., *Connecticut Divorces: Superior Court Records for the Counties of Litchfield, 1752–1922, and Hartford, 1740–1849* (Bowie, Md.: Heritage Books, 1989), 11–31. See the bibliography for a complete listing of Connecticut and Vermont newspapers used in this study.

17. Equity jurisprudence was far more complex than I have indicated in this very brief description. For a brief, but thorough, explanation of equity, see Lebsock, *The Free Women of Petersburg,* 54–86. Marylynn Salmon, *Women and the Law of Property,* 6–11, 81–140, provides an excellent analysis of equity proceedings in courts of chancery and of the reasons for and the effects of the lack of chancery courts in New England. Salmon maintains that because New England did not have separate chancery courts, the administration of equity in these states lagged behind that of other sections of the United States. In her analysis of Connecticut court decisions regarding married women's separate estates, Salmon demonstrates the existence of "a poor understanding of equitable principles among even the most distinguished members of the Connecticut bar" (131). On chancery courts allowing estranged wives to control their separate estates, see Salmon, 91.

18. Gilmore, *Reading Becomes a Necessity,* 119–21; David D. Hall, *Worlds of Wonder, Days of Judgment: Popular Religious Belief in Early New England* (New York: Knopf, 1989), chapter 1; Kenneth Lockridge, *Literacy in Colonial New England* (New York: Norton, 1974); E. Jennifer Monaghan, "Literacy Instruction and Gender in Colonial New England," *American Quarterly* 40, no. 1 (1988): 18–41.

19. Because there are occasional gaps in extant newspapers, it is possible that some of these twelve women were responding to husbands' notices, but that evidence of the men's advertisements has not survived.

NOTES TO CHAPTER I

1. Martin Tullar, *A Concise System of Family Duty* (Windsor, Vt., 1802), 11–13, 33, 34, 36, 39, 40. For an excellent discussion of Puritan ideals concerning wives, see Laurel Thatcher Ulrich, *Good Wives: Image and Reality in the Lives of Women in Northern New England, 1650–1750* (New York: Vintage Books, 1980).

2. Tullar, *A Concise System,* 6, 15, 27.

3. William Jay, *The Mutual Duties of Husbands and Wives* (Boston, 1808), 12.

4. Works that analyze married women's legal and economic subordination to their husbands include Norma Basch, *In the Eyes of the Law: Women, Marriage, and Property in Nineteenth-Century New York* (Ithaca, N.Y.: Cornell University Press, 1982); Jeanne Boydston, *Home and Work: Housework, Wages, and the Ideology of Labor in the Early Republic* (New York: Oxford University Press, 1990); Nancy F. Cott, "Divorce and the Changing Status of Women in Eighteenth-Century Massachusetts," *William and Mary Quarterly*, 3rd series, 33, no. 4 (1976): 586–614; Nancy F. Cott, *The Bonds of Womanhood: "Woman's Sphere" in New England, 1785–1830* (New Haven, Conn.: Yale University Press, 1977); Linda K. Kerber, *Women of the Republic: Intellect and Ideology in Revolutionary America* (Chapel Hill: University of North Carolina Press, 1980); Marylynn Salmon, *Women and the Law of Property in Early America* (Chapel Hill: University of North Carolina Press, 1986); Ulrich, *Good Wives*; and Laurel Thatcher Ulrich, *A Midwife's Tale: The Life of Martha Ballard, Based on Her Diary, 1785–1812* (New York: Vintage Books, 1990). On the development of the companionate marriage ideal in the early national period, see Carl N. Degler, *At Odds: Women and the Family in America from the Revolution to the Present* (New York: Oxford University Press, 1980), chapter 1; Anya Jabour, *Marriage in the Early Republic: Elizabeth and William Wirt and the Companionate Ideal* (Baltimore: Johns Hopkins University Press, 1998); Jan Lewis, "The Republican Wife: Virtue and Seduction in the Early Republic," *William and Mary Quarterly*, 3rd series, 44, no. 4 (October 1987): 689–721; and Merril D. Smith, *Breaking the Bonds: Marital Discord in Pennsylvania, 1730–1830* (New York: New York University Press, 1991), especially chapter 2. For attitudes toward and social policy on violence within marriage, see Elizabeth Pleck, *Domestic Tyranny: The Making of American Social Policy against Family Violence from Colonial Times to the Present* (New York: Oxford University Press, 1987); the essays in Christine Daniels and Michael V. Kennedy, eds., *Over the Threshold: Intimate Violence in Early America* (New York: Routledge Press, 1999), especially Randolph A. Roth, "Spousal Murder in Northern New England, 1776–1865," 65–93; and Christine Stansell, *City of Women: Sex and Class in New York, 1789–1860* (Urbana: University of Illinois Press, 1987), 29–30, 78–83.

5. William Kenrick, *The Whole Duty of Woman* (Windsor, Vt., 1792), 53; "Hints Tending to Promote and Secure Happiness in the Married State," *The Weekly Visitor, or Ladies' Miscellany* [New York], 11 February 1804; *Mirror* [Middlebury, Vt.], 26 March 1806; "Matrimonial Maxims," *Vermont Republican* [Windsor, Vt.], 16 June 1827.

6. Cott, *The Bonds of Womanhood*, 80–83; Ellen K. Rothman, *Hands and Hearts: A History of Courtship in America* (Cambridge: Harvard University Press, 1987), 61–73, also discusses the hesitation with which young women approached marriage in the early national period. Lee Virginia Chambers-Schiller,

Liberty a Better Husband: Single Women in America: The Generations of 1780–1840 (New Haven, Conn.: Yale University Press, 1984), argues that in the early republic, increasing numbers of American women pursued individual liberty and personal autonomy by remaining unmarried.

7. "Essay on Marriage," *The New York Weekly Magazine* [New York], 22 March 1797; James Bean, *The Christian Minister's Affectionate Advice to a Married Couple* (Boston, 1815), 36; "A Pair of Matrimonial Portraits," *Watchman* [Montpelier, Vt.], 13 May 1808.

8. Esther Kimball, *National Standard* [Middlebury, Vt.], 18 December 1821; VRSV, 1760–1870, GSCSV, microfilm.

9. Bean, *The Christian Minister's Affectionate Advice,* 36; "On Marriage," *South Carolina Weekly Museum* [Charleston, S.C.], 27 May 1797; William Giles, *The Guide to Domestic Happiness* (New Haven, Conn., 1804), 123; John Angell James, *The Family Monitor; or, A Help to Domestic Happiness* (Boston, 1829), 57.

10. Jay, *The Mutual Duties of Husbands and Wives,* 11–12; Anon., *The Wife* (Boston, 1806), 11.

11. Zebulon Huntington, *Windsor* [Vt.] *Federal Gazette,* 12 July 1803; Ammi Andrews, *Vermont Journal* [Windsor, Vt.], 1 September 1797. For more information on the Shakers, see Stephen J. Stein, *The Shaker Experience in America* (New Haven, Conn.: Yale University Press, 1992). Mary Beth Norton, "'My Resting Reaping Times': Sarah Osborne's Defense of Her Unfeminine Activities, 1767," *Signs* 2, no. 2 (1976): 515–29, and Lyle Koehler, "The Case of the American Jezebels: Anne Hutchinson and Female Agitation during the Years of the Antinomian Turmoil, 1636–1640," *William and Mary Quarterly,* 3rd series, 31, no. 1 (1974): 55–78, both explore the tensions between Puritan religious beliefs and gender roles, as manifested in the activities of Hutchinson and Osborne. Elizabeth A. De Wolfe, *Shaking the Faith: Women, Family, and Mary Marshall Dyer's Anti-Shaker Campaign, 1815–1867* (New York: Palgrave, 2002), analyzes marital conflict that occurred when one spouse adhered to the Shaker sect and the other did not.

12. Chester Wright, *Jesus Weeping at Lazarus's Grave: A Sermon, Preached at Montpelier, Dec. 17, 1813, at the Burial of Mrs. Hannah Loomis, Wife of Jeduthan Loomis, Esquire* (Montpelier, Vt., 1814), 10; Asa Burton, *A Sermon, Preached at the Funeral of Mrs. Joanna Shaw, Consort of Colonel Dan Shaw* (Hanover, N.H., 1804), 17; Isaiah Parker, *A Funeral Discourse, the Substance of Which Was Delivered in Cavendish: At the Interment of Mrs. Esther Chaplin, Wife of Capt. William Chaplin* (Harvard, Mass., 1807), 26–27.

13. Bean, *The Christian Minister's Affectionate Advice,* 14; Charles W. Peale, *An Essay to Promote Domestic Happiness* (Philadelphia, Pa., 1812), 17.

14. Anon., *The Wife,* 81; Warren Skinner, *Influence of the Female Character:*

A Sermon on the Importance and Influence of Female Character (Cavendish, Vt., [182?]), n.p.; "Hints for Young Married Women," *The American Museum* [Philadelphia, Pa.], December 1789.

15. "Matrimonial Maxims," *Vermont Republican,* 16 June 1827; "Female Influence," *Green Mountain Patriot* [Peacham, Vt.], 16 May 1799; "Woman!" *Vermont Centinel* [Burlington, Vt.], 20 February 1824; Jay, *The Mutual Duties,* 12.

16. Skinner, *Influence of the Female Character,* 13; Tullar, *A Concise System,* 20, 27. Lewis, "The Republican Wife," also points out that while prescriptive and fictional writers presented an exalted view of wives' ability to influence their husbands for the good, they uniformly advised wives to defer to their husbands to avoid marital conflicts.

17. James Kent, *Commentaries on American Law,* 4 vols. (1826, rpt. Boston, 1884), 1:228. See also William Blackstone, *Commentaries on the Laws of England,* 2 vols. (1765–1769, rpt. New York, 1836), 1:355–66. Kerber, *Women of the Republic,* 139–55, provides an excellent discussion of the implications of *feme covert* status.

18. Tapping Reeve, *The Law of Baron and Feme, of Parent and Child, Guardian and Ward, Master and Servant,* (1816, rpt. Albany, N.Y., 1862), 141–42.

19. Zephaniah Swift, *Digest of the Laws of the State of Connecticut,* 2 vols. (New Haven, Conn.: 1822), 1:25; Kent, *Commentaries,* 2:157.

20. Swift, *Digest,* 1:40. Oliver Williams, *Connecticut Courant* [Hartford, Conn.], 15 February 1814; Timothy Wood, *Connecticut Courant,* 1 August 1791; Nathaniel Jewett, *Vermont Journal,* 7 May 1805; Timothy Kittredge, *Vermont Journal,* 8 October 1799; Jeremiah Perrin, *Connecticut Courant,* 13 September, 1802.

21. Henry Gould, *Rutland* [Vt.] *Herald,* 22 January 1817; Abraham Holmes, *Vermont Centinel,* 20 September 1822; Samuel Bigelow, *Vermont Gazette* [Bennington, Vt.], 27 July 1792. Joan R. Gundersen, "Independence, Citizenship, and the American Revolution," *Signs* 13, no. 1 (1987): 59–77, argues that the heightened importance placed on independence in the Revolutionary era highlighted women's lack of independence. She claims that men "could enhance their independence by stressing the dependence of others (including women) on them." Placing desertion notices emphasized men's position as independent heads of households who were responsible for maintaining and controlling their dependents.

22. John Miller, *Connecticut Courant,* 27 March 1797; Parker Chapy, *Vermont Journal,* 27 October 1817, 5 January 1818.

23. Abigail Pell, *Green Mountain Patriot,* 9 July 1805; Chloe Ames, *Vermont Journal,* 10 December 1799; Betsey Lewis, *National Standard,* 8 January 1817.

24. The most common complaint in both Vermont and Connecticut women's

postings was that their husbands had failed to provide for them economically (57 percent in Vermont; 67 percent in Connecticut). Approximately one-third of women in both states complained that their husbands had deserted (the second most common complaint in Connecticut, the third most common in Vermont). Approximately 15 percent of Vermont women and 20 percent of Connecticut women complained that their husbands had committed adultery. With the addition of cruelty, these complaints were the most common and statistically significant ones that appeared in women's postings.

25. The original Connecticut divorce statute is quoted in Kerber, *Women of the Republic,* 161. For the changes made in 1846, see *The Revised Statutes of the State of Connecticut* (Hartford, Conn., 1849), 274.

26. William Slade, ed., *Vermont State Papers* (Middlebury, Vt., 1825), 264; *Statutes of the State of Vermont* (Bennington, Vt., 1791), 50; William Slade, ed., *The Laws of Vermont of a Publick and Permanent Nature: Coming Down to and including the Year 1824* (Windsor, Vt., 1825), 363. Vermont's and Connecticut's divorce statutes were more liberal than laws in Massachusetts, New York, and the southern states. Massachusetts's 1786 divorce law, which allowed divorce on the grounds of consanguinity, bigamy, impotence, or adultery, appears in Cott, "Divorce and the Changing Status of Women," 612; the New York statute, which allowed for divorce only on the grounds of adultery, appears in Norma Basch, "Relief in the Premises: Divorce as a Woman's Remedy in New York and Indiana, 1815–1870," *Law and History Review* 8, no. 1 (1990): 3. Until the 1830s, divorce in southern states could be obtained only by legislative decree. Jane Turner Censer, "'Smiling through Her Tears': Ante-Bellum Southern Women and Divorce," *American Journal of Legal History* 25 (January 1981): 24–47. The Connecticut law was similar to the laws of Pennsylvania and Tennessee. Pennsylvania's Divorce Act (1785) and Tennessee's 1799 statute allowed total divorce for adultery, bigamy, impotence, and desertion; Pennsylvania and Tennessee also provided for court-ordered separations (but not total divorce) on the grounds of cruelty. Smith, *Breaking the Bonds,* 24; Lawrence B. Goodheart, Neil Hanks, Elizabeth Johnson, "'An Act for the Relief of Females . . .': Divorce and the Changing Legal Status of Women in Tennessee, 1796–1860, Part 1," *Tennessee Historical Quarterly* 44, no. 3 (1985): 320, 321. Vermont law was most similar to Rhode Island's 1798 statute and Ohio's 1803 law, which gave courts the power to grant divorces on the grounds of adultery, bigamy, impotence, desertion, and cruelty. Sheldon S. Cohen, "The Broken Bond: Divorce in Providence County, 1749–1809," *Rhode Island History* 44 (August 1985): 68; Martin Schultz, "Divorce in Early America: Origins and Patterns in Three North Central States," *Sociological Quarterly* 25 (April 1984): 517. As in most other states during this time period, the Vermont Supreme Court and Connecticut Superior Court "rode" a circuit, sitting twice a year in each county. Vermont Supreme Court records exist on microfilm at the VSL for Windsor County be-

tween February 1794 and June 1825, for Chittenden County between January 1800 and January 1834, and for Washington County between September 1821 and March 1829. Connecticut Superior Court Divorce Records exist for Hartford County between 1740 and 1849. HCDR, 1740–1849, CSL, microfilm; Barbara B. Ferris and Grace Louise Knox, compilers, *Connecticut Divorces: Superior Court Records for the Counties of Litchfield, 1752–1922, and Hartford, 1740–1849* (Bowie, Md.: Heritage Books, 1989), 11–31.

27. There are forty-eight such extant petitions; the assembly granted thirty-four of them. CALD, vols. 1 and 2, Index, CSL, microfilm.

28. Cornelia Hughes Dayton argues that behind Connecticut legislators' "reluctance to admit cruelty to the list of grounds [for divorce] was an unwillingness to cede to women a significant measure of power in determining the limits to male authority in marriage" in *Women before the Bar: Gender, Law, and Society in Connecticut, 1639–1789* (Chapel Hill: University of North Carolina Press, 1995), 115. Roth, "Spousal Murder," argues that marital homicide, one indicator of rates of violence within marriages, was lower in northern New England than in other sections of the country because of legal support for abused spouses, the willingness of neighbors and other family members to intervene, and popular attitudes that condemned violence within marriage.

29. These statistics are drawn from an analysis of divorce petitions presented to the Vermont Supreme Court while it sat in Chittenden County between 1800 and 1830, in Washington County between 1821 and 1829, and in Windsor County between 1794 and 1825; petitions presented to the Connecticut Superior Court while it sat in Hartford County between 1790 and 1830; and petitions presented to the Connecticut Assembly between 1789 and 1820. VSCR, VSL, microfilm; HCDR, CSL, microfilm; Ferris and Knox, comps., *Connecticut Divorces,* 11–31; CALD, CSL, microfilm.

30. Norma Basch makes a similar point about men's ability to end their marriages with de facto divorces and women's need to turn to the legal system to obtain the same end in "Relief in the Premises," 8, 16. For works that emphasize a connection between improvements in women's status and access to divorce, see Cott, "Divorce and the Changing Status of Women"; Degler, *At Odds*; Steven Mintz and Susan Kellogg, *Domestic Revolutions: A Social History of American Family Life* (New York: Free Press, 1988); Glenda Riley, *Divorce: An American Tradition* (New York: Oxford University Press, 1991); and Smith, *Breaking the Bonds.*

31. "On Divorce," *National Recorder* [Philadelphia, Pa.], 31 July 1819. Michael Grossberg, *Governing the Hearth: Law and the Family in Nineteenth-Century America* (Chapel Hill: University of North Carolina Press, 1985), 301, argues that by substituting the authority of a male judiciary for that of husbands, more liberal divorce laws did not truly threaten male patriarchal authority within marriage. Lawrence B. Goodheart, Neil Hanks, and Elizabeth Johnson

argue that divorce protected patriarchal marriage by offering women a safety valve to escape their husbands' abuses in "'An Act for the Relief of Females . . .': Divorce and the Changing Legal Status of Women in Tennessee, 1796, 1860, Part 2," *Tennessee Historical Quarterly* 44, no. 4 (1985): 410. Of course, the fact that divorce proponents did not intend divorce on the grounds of cruelty to threaten marital patriarchy did not mean that those men whose wives successfully divorced them on these grounds believed that their authority remained unchallenged. See Mary Beth Sievens, "Divorce, Patriarchal Authority, and Masculinity: A Case from Early National Vermont," *Journal of Social History* 37, no. 3 (2004): 651–61.

32. *Phebe Huston v. Thomas Huston,* VSCR, Chittenden County, January 1813, VSL, microfilm.

33. Esther Woodbury, *North Star* [Danville, Vt.], 24 June 1809; Anna Norris, *North Star,* 25 July 1817; *Rachel Nichols v. Joseph Nichols,* VSCR, Chittenden County, January 1805, VSL, microfilm. Kent, *Commentaries,* 2:157. In "The Evolution of the Doctrine of Mental Cruelty in Victorian American Divorce, 1790–1900," *Journal of Social History* 20, no. 1 (1986): 127–48, Robert L. Griswold traces the gradual acceptance of mental cruelty, such as threats, as grounds for divorce. According to Griswold, after 1880 some jurisdictions began to claim that mental cruelty was sufficient grounds for divorce.

34. Thirty-six Connecticut women petitioned the assembly for divorce on the sole grounds of cruelty. Twenty-five were successful. Of the eleven women who petitioned on the grounds of cruelty in combination with another complaint, nine were successful. *Petition of Ruth Shelton,* April 1796, CALD, Vol. 2, Index, 22, CSL, microfilm. *Petition of Eunice Bird,* May 1797, CALD, Vol. 1, 30, CSL, microfilm.

35. *Ruby Gleason v. Thomas Gleason,* VSCR, Windsor County, June 1824, VSL, microfilm; *Petition of Sarah Arnold,* CALD, Vol. I, 3, CSL, microfilm.

36. *Rebecca Newell v. William Newell,* VSCR, Chittenden County, January 1826, VSL, microfilm.

NOTES TO CHAPTER 2

1. Uriah Hayes, *Vermont Republican* [Windsor, Vt.], 11 October 1813; VRSV, 1760–1870, GSCSV, microfilm; *Rachel Hayes v. Uriah Hayes,* VSCR, Windsor County, February 1819, VSL, microfilm; *Rachel Hayes v. Uriah Hayes,* WCCR, September 1823, Vol. 13, 414, BHL, microfilm; Pomfret, Vermont, Land Records, Vol. 6, 239–40, Vol. 7, 147, 193, 529, GSCSV, microfilm; *John Finney v. Rachel Hayes,* WCCR, March 1824, Vol. 13, 440, BHL, microfilm.

2. For married women's legal status in the early republic, see Norma Basch, *In the Eyes of the Law: Women, Marriage, and Property in Nineteenth-Century New York* (Ithaca, N.Y.: Cornell University Press, 1982); Linda K. Kerber,

Women of the Republic: Intellect and Ideology in Revolutionary America (Chapel Hill: University of North Carolina Press, 1980); Marylynn Salmon, *Women and the Law of Property in Early America* (Chapel Hill: University of North Carolina Press, 1986). For the tensions between traditional patriarchal society and women's opportunities to act in their own interests within that society, see Laurel Thatcher Ulrich, *Good Wives: Image and Reality in the Lives of Women in Northern New England, 1650–1750* (New York: Vintage Books, 1980); and Laurel Thatcher Ulrich, *A Midwife's Tale: The Life of Martha Ballard, Based on Her Diary, 1785–1812* (New York: Vintage Books, 1990).

3. James Kent, *Commentaries on American Law*, 4 vols. (1826; rpt. Boston, 1884), 2:184; William Blackstone, *Commentaries on the Laws of England*, 2 vols. (1765–1769, rpt. New York, 1836), 1:356–59.

4. Kent, *Commentaries*, 2:229; Richard Hills, *American Mercury* [Hartford, Conn.], 27 September 1804; Rufus Baldwin, *Vermont Journal* [Windsor, Vt.], 16 February 1801; Jesse Moon, *Rutland* [Vt.] *Herald*, 12 December 1820.

5. Jesse Root, ed., *Reports of Cases Adjudged in the Superior Court and in the Supreme Court of Errors in the State of Connecticut from June A.D. 1793, to January A.D. 1798*, 2 vols. (Hartford: State of Connecticut, 1962), 2:468–69. In its written opinion, the court dismissed the issue of Frances Sistare's Spanish citizenship as irrelevant. Only her refusal to live with her husband prohibited her from claiming her dower right in his estate.

6. William Hector, *Connecticut Courant* [Hartford, Conn.], 26 October 1795; Thomas Sloan, *American Mercury*, 25 May 1795; Nathan Kinne, *North Star* [Danville, Vt.], 25 December 1827. Fifteen percent of Connecticut husbands and 18 percent of Vermont men specifically mentioned in their notices the unreasonable debts their wives had contracted (or had threatened to contract).

7. Kent, *Commentaries*, 2:185. Thirty-one percent of Vermont women and 33 percent of Connecticut wives who wrote elopement notices denied that they had deserted. Sally Meigs, *Rutland Herald*, 5 December 1796; Amy Hammond, *Vermont Journal*, 16 August 1791.

8. Tapping Reeve, *The Law of Baron and Feme, of Parent and Child, Guardian and Ward, Master and Servant, and of the Powers of the Courts of Chancery* (1816, rpt. Albany, N.Y., 1862), 160; Anna Crosby, *Connecticut Courant*, 28 July 1800; Sarah Church, *Vermont Journal*, 9 May 1814.

9. William Blanchard, *Argus* [Putney, Vt.], 9 August 1798; Anna Blanchard, *Argus*, 18 August 1798.

10. Kent, *Commentaries*, 2:187; Reeve, *The Law of Baron and Feme*, 158; Samuel Cesar, *Vermont Gazette* [Bennington, Vt.], 29 March 1802; Phebe Cesar, *Vermont Gazette*, 12 April 1802.

11. For works on the consumer revolution in the British North American colonies and in the United States, see T. H. Breen, "An Empire of Goods: The

Anglicization of Colonial America, 1690–1776," *Journal of British Studies* 25, no. 4 (1986): 476–99; T. H. Breen, "Baubles of Britain: The American and Consumer Revolution of the Eighteenth Century," *Past and Present* 119 (May 1988): 73–104; Richard Bushman, *The Refinement of America: Persons, Houses, Cities* (New York: Knopf, 1992).

12. The literature on the economic transformation of the New England countryside is large and growing. See, for example, Christopher Clark, "Household Economy, Market Exchange and the Rise of Capitalism in the Connecticut Valley, 1800–1860," *Journal of Social History* 13, no. 2 (1979): 169–89; Christopher Clark, *The Roots of Rural Capitalism: Western Massachusetts, 1780–1860* (Ithaca, N.Y.: Cornell University Press, 1990); Robert A. Gross, "Culture and Cultivation: Agriculture and Society in Thoreau's Concord," *Journal of American History* 69, no. 1 (1982): 42–55; David Jaffee, "Peddlers of Progress and the Transformation of the Rural North, 1760–1860," *Journal of American History* 78, no. 2 (1991): 511–35; David Jaffee, "The Village Enlightenment in New England, 1760–1820," *William and Mary Quarterly*, 3rd series, 47 (July 1990): 327–46; David Jaffee, "One of the Primitive Sort: Portrait Makers in the Rural North, 1760–1860," in Steven Hahn and Jonathan Prude, eds., *The Countryside in the Age of the Capitalist Transformation: Essays in the Social History of Rural America* (Chapel Hill: University of North Carolina Press, 1985): 103–38. Jeanne Boydston, *Home and Work: Housework, Wages, and the Ideology of Labor in the Early Republic* (New York: Oxford University Press, 1990); Nancy F. Cott, *The Bonds of Womanhood: "Woman's Sphere" in New England, 1785–1835* (New Haven, Conn.: Yale University Press, 1977), 19–62; Anya Jabour, *Marriage in the Early Republic: Elizabeth and William Wirt and the Companionate Ideal* (Baltimore: Johns Hopkins University Press, 1998); Joan Jensen, *Loosening the Bonds: Mid-Atlantic Farm Women, 1750–1850* (New Haven, Conn.: Yale University Press, 1986); Catherine E. Kelly, *In the New England Fashion: Reshaping Women's Lives in the Nineteenth Century* (Ithaca, N.Y.: Cornell University Press, 1999), 19–63; and Mary P. Ryan, *Cradle of the Middle Class: The Family in Oneida County, New York, 1790–1865* (Cambridge: Cambridge University Press, 1981), all analyze the transformation of women's work in response to the economic changes of the late eighteenth and early nineteenth centuries.

13. These examples from merchants' advertisements were drawn from the *Vermont Republican*, 16 June 1827, and the *Vermont Journal*, 3 January, 1792, 9 August 1828.

14. Lance E. Davis, et al., *American Economic Growth: An Economist's History of the United States* (New York: HarperCollins, 1972), 25, 419–37, 562–81. Cathy Matson, "The Revolution, the Constitution, and the New Nation," in Stanley L. Engerman and Robert E. Gallman, eds., *The Cambridge Economic*

History of the United States, 3 vols. (Cambridge: Cambridge University Press, 1996): 1:363–401. Thanks to Stacey Helmbrecht-Wilson for this information and these citations.

15. A classic analysis of the relationship between economic change, social transformation, and marital dissolution is Paul E. Johnson, "The Modernization of Mayo Greenleaf Patch: Land, Family, and Marginality in New England, 1766–1818," *New England Quarterly* 55, no. 4 (1982): 488–516. David Shaw, *Connecticut Courant,* 22 April 1793; Petition of David Shaw, Connecticut Archives, Series 2, Insolvent Debtors, 1750–1820, Vol. 11, 27, CSL, microfilm; Daikis Shaw, *Connecticut Courant,* 12 May 1812.

16. "On Matrimony," *Green Mountain Patriot* [Peacham, Vt.], 29 October 1800; "A Clergyman's Address to Married Persons at the Altar," *New England Farmer* [Boston, Mass.], 28 June 1823; Anon., *Advice in Order to Prevent Poverty; To Which Is Added Directions to a Young Tradesman. Written by an Old One* (Windsor, Vt., 1792), 10; Charles W. Peale, *An Essay to Promote Domestic Happiness* (Philadelphia, 1812), 18.

17. "Letter of Marriage," *The American Museum* [Philadelphia], January 1788; "Celibacy," *North Star,* 16 October 1827. For a discussion of women's growing responsibility for family consumption, see Boydston, *Home and Work;* Cott, *The Bonds of Womanhood,* 19–62; Jabour, *Marriage in the Early Republic;* and Ryan, *Cradle of the Middle Class,* 200–203. Donna DeFabio Curtin, "'The *Gentlest,* the Most *Polished,* Most *Beautiful* Part of the Creation': Gender and Gentility in the Early Republic," paper presented at the annual meeting of the Society for Historians of the Early American Republic, Cincinnati, Ohio, July 1995, counts fifty articles in the *American Museum* between 1787 and 1792 that examine the ill effects of women's consumption on society, the family, and the republic. Alan Taylor, "The Gendered Order of a Rural Village in the Early American Republic" (unpublished paper), 15, also notes that the newspapers of Otsego County, New York, were filled with essays complaining about women's consumer activities in the 1790s and 1800s. Stacy Helmbrecht-Wilson, "'Went a Shopping': Elite and Middling Women as Consumers in Massachusetts, 1790–1830" (Ph.D. diss., Boston University, 1999), analyzes Massachusetts newspaper essays decrying women's frivolous consumer activity as harmful to their families and the republic. She argues that "the overblown denunciations of the articles helped Americans exorcise their fears about the transformation occurring in women's roles as consumers and the larger social and economic changes taking place. The extravagance and extreme hyperbole of the articles' accusations allowed Americans to see the actual changes occurring in their lives as reasonable and moderate" (5–6).

18. Edward Barney, *American Yeoman* [Brattleboro, Vt.], 11 February 1817.

19. Jacob Ames, Jr., *Vermont Journal,* 5 November 1799; Chloe Ames, *Vermont Journal,* 10 December 1799.

20. Elias Hall, *A Disclosure of Facts, in Consequence of a Decree for Alimony; By the Supreme Court, Addison County, January Term, 1823, against Elias Hall* (Montpelier, Vt., 1825), 39, 43; John Priest, *Messenger* [Brattleboro, Vt.], 1 April 1826; Calvin Preston, *Connecticut Courant,* 15 August 1791; Nathaniel Smith, *Vermont Gazette,* 2 August 1798.

21. *Justin & Elias Lyman v. Uriah Hayes,* Windsor Superior Court Civil Case Judgments, 1813–1814, GSCSV.

22. Deposition of Hannah Brownell, *Justin & Elias Lyman v. Uriah Hayes.*

23. Deposition of Hannah Brownell, *Justin & Elias Lyman v. Uriah Hayes.*

24. *Justin & Elias Lyman v. Uriah Hayes; Rachel Hayes v. Uriah Hayes,* VSCR, Windsor County, February 1819, VSL, microfilm.

25. Zephaniah Swift, *Digest of the Laws of the State of Connecticut,* 2 vols. (New Haven, Conn., 1822), 1:31, 1:33.

26. Asa Aikens, *Reports of Cases Argued and Determined in the Supreme Court of the State of Vermont,* 2 vols. (Windsor, Vt., 1827) 1:174–79.

27. Aikens, *Reports,* 1:177, 1:179.

28. *Fanny Gladding v. James Gladding,* HCDR, January 1823, CSL, microfilm.

NOTES TO CHAPTER 3

1. Asa Goodenow, *Rutland Herald,* 23 March 1795.

2. Jeanne Boydston, *Home and Work: Housework, Wages, and the Ideology of Labor in the Early Republic* (New York: Oxford University Press, 1990), 116–19, 153–59.

3. Jeanne Boydston, "The Woman Who Wasn't There: Women's Market Labor and the Transition to Capitalism in the United States," *Journal of the Early Republic* 16, no. 2 (1996): 183–206.

4. According to the 1820 Census, 7,491 Hartford County residents (66%) labored in agriculture; 799 (7%) in commerce; and 3,028 (27%) in manufacturing. In Windsor County, 7,305 residents (83%) labored in agriculture; 138 (1.5%) in commerce; and 1,368 (15.5%) in manufacturing. United States Fourth Census, 1820, Connecticut, Vermont.

5. On the Vermont economy, see Hal S. Barron, *Those Who Stayed Behind: Rural Society in Nineteenth-Century New England* (Cambridge: Cambridge University Press, 1984); Randolph A. Roth, *The Democratic Dilemma: Religion, Reform, and the Social Order in the Connecticut River Valley of Vermont, 1791–1850* (Cambridge: Cambridge University Press, 1987); and Lewis Stilwell, *Migration from Vermont (1791–1860)* (Montpelier: Vermont Historical Society, 1948). On the Connecticut economy, see Richard Bushman, *From Puritan to Yankee: Character and the Social Order in Connecticut, 1690–1765* (Cambridge: Harvard University Press, 1967), and Bruce C. Daniels, *The Connecticut*

Town: Growth and Development, 1635–1790 (Middletown, Conn.: Wesleyan University Press, 1979). On the New England economy in general, see Christopher Clark, *The Roots of Rural Capitalism: Western Massachusetts, 1780–1860* (Ithaca, N.Y.: Cornell University Press, 1990); and Howard S. Russell, *A Long Deep Furrow: Three Centuries of Farming in New England* (Hanover, N.H.: University Press of New England, 1982).

6. VRSV, 1760–1870, GSCSV, microfilm; Hartford District Probate Records, Vol. 29, 218, GSCSV, microfilm; Evelyn M. Wood Lovejoy, *History of Royalton, Vermont, with Family Genealogies, 1769–1911* (Burlington, Vt.: Free Press Printing Co., 1911); Royalton, Vermont, Deeds, Vol. D, 171, 446; E, 142; F, 131, 353, GSCSV, microfilm; *Connecticut Courant* [Hartford, Conn.], 28 July 1800.

7. Ira Allen, *The Natural and Political History of the State of Vermont* (London, 1798), 165.

8. Charles G. Eastman (1816–1860), "A Picture," Vermont Broadsides, American Antiquarian Society, Worcester, Mass. For the gendered division of labor in northern rural households, see Boydston, *Home and Work*; John Mack Faragher, *Women and Men on the Overland Trail* (New Haven, Conn.: Yale University Press, 1979), 40–65; Joan M. Jensen, *Loosening the Bonds: Mid-Atlantic Farm Women, 1750–1850* (New Haven, Conn.: Yale University Press, 1986); and Nancy Grey Osterud, *Bonds of Community: The Lives of Farm Women in Nineteenth-Century New York* (Ithaca, N.Y.: Cornell University Press, 1991).

9. Joseph O. Goodwin, *East Hartford: Its History and Traditions* (1879, rpt. East Hartford: Raymond Library Co., 1976), 160–61; Frank D. Andrews, ed., *BusinessMen of the City of Hartford (Connecticut) in the Year 1799* (Vineland, N.J.: F. D. Andrews, 1909), CSL, microfilm; Frank D. Andrews, ed., *Directory for the City of Hartford for the Year 1799* (Vineland, N.J.: F. D. Andrews, 1910), CSL, microfilm; *The Pocket Register for the City of Hartford* (Hartford, Conn., 1825), CSL, microfilm; *Hartford City Directory for 1828* (Hartford, Conn., 1828), CSL, microfilm.

10. Lewis Cass Aldrich and Frank R. Holmes, eds., *History of Windsor County* (Syracuse, N.Y., 1891), 314; William J. Gilmore, *Reading Becomes a Necessity of Life: Material and Cultural Life in Rural New England, 1780–1835* (Knoxville: University of Tennessee Press, 1989), 32, 92, 93, 394.

11. On the economic strategies of working-class wives and the wives of small urban producers, see Christine Stansell, *City of Women: Sex and Class in New York, 1789–1860* (Urbana: University of Illinois Press, 1987), 3–18, 46–52. Boydston, *Home and Work*; Catherine E. Kelly, *In the New England Fashion: Reshaping Women's Lives in the Nineteenth Century* (Ithaca, N.Y.: Cornell University Press, 1999); and Mary P. Ryan, *Cradle of the Middle Class: The Family in Oneida County, New York, 1790–1865* (Cambridge: Cambridge University

Press, 1981), address middle-class economic strategies. Anya Jabour, *Marriage in the Early Republic: Elizabeth and William Wirt and the Companionate Ideal* (Baltimore: Johns Hopkins University Press, 1998), 25–36, 59–73, 100–114, examines the changing economic strategies of the Wirt family, residents of several southern cities in the early national period. Jabour chronicles the Wirts' move from a partnership in which Elizabeth was responsible for domestic production to an almost complete reliance on William's wages to supply the family's needs.

12. Nineteen percent of Vermont men and 22 percent of Connecticut men included this complaint in their postings.

13. Ezra Dunham, *Rutland Herald,* 28 July 1804; Petition of James Gladding, HCDR, February 1821, CSL, microfilm; Moses Rood, *Connecticut Courant,* 4 May 1819; John Roberts, *Gazette* [Poultney, Vt.], 10 July 1823.

14. Nathan Foster, *Vermont Intelligencer* [Bellows Falls, Vt.], 25 November 1822; Joseph Lovel, *Weekly Wanderer* [Randolph, Vt.], 23 July 1804; Elias Hall, *A Disclosure of Facts, in Consequence of a Decree for Alimony by the Supreme Court, Addison County, January Term, 1823, against Elias Hall* (Montpelier, Vt., 1825), 44, 45, 48.

15. Curtis Hale, *Vermont Centinel* [Rutland, Vt.], 13 August 1806; Edward Wood, *Connecticut Courant,* 10 April 1797; Jason Perkins, *Connecticut Courant,* 19 April 1814; Samuel Jones, *Rutland Herald,* 3 December 1821.

16. Robert Bloomer, *Vermont Gazette* [Bennington, Vt.], 12 January 1801; James Kent, *Commentaries on American Law,* 4 vols. (1826, rpt. Boston, 1884), 2:229.

17. In their desertion notices, 57 percent of Vermont women and 66 percent of Connecticut wives accused their husbands of failing to provide economic support. Sixty-seven percent of Vermont women and 69 percent of Connecticut wives petitioned for divorce on the grounds of desertion, which, by definition, meant that their husbands had failed to provide them with support.

18. Rachel Martin, *Mirror* [Middlebury, Vt.], 13 July 1803; Petition of Lucretia Hill, HCDR, February 1826, CSL, microfilm; Tabitha Austens, *Argus* [Putney, Vt.], 16 March 1797.

19. Elizabeth Hamblin, *Green Mountain Farmer* [Bennington, Vt.], 17 July 1809.

20. Hannah West, *Vermont Journal* [Windsor, Vt.], 5 August 1811; Betty Bandel also quotes West and comments on her characterization of her household labors in "What the Good Laws of Men Hath Put Asunder . . ." *Vermont History* 46, no. 4 (1978): 221–33.

21. Lucy Martin, *Vermont Gazette,* 3 April 1795; Sarah Hall, *American Mercury* [Hartford, Conn.], 23 December 1802; Clarissa Post, *American Mercury,* 8 October 1816; Sarah Church, *Vermont Journal,* 9 May 1814.

22. Esther Green, *Connecticut Courant,* 20 July 1813.

23. For works that note the connections among women's productive labors, neighborly exchange, and the market, see Clark, *The Roots of Rural Capitalism*; Jensen, *Loosening the Bonds*; Kelly, *In the New England Fashion*, 19–63; Osterud, *Bonds of Community*; Laurel Thatcher Ulrich, "Housewife and Gadder: Themes of Self-Sufficiency and Community in Eighteenth-Century New England," in Carol Groneman and Mary Beth Norton, eds., *"To Toil the Livelong Day": America's Women at Work, 1780–1980* (Ithaca, N.Y.: Cornell University Press, 1987), 21–34; Laurel Thatcher Ulrich, "'A Friendly Neighbor': Social Dimensions of Daily Work in Northern Colonial New England," in Kathryn Kish Sklar and Thomas Dublin, eds., *Women and Power in American History: A Reader*. vol. 1, *To 1800* (Englewood Cliffs, N.J.: Prentice Hall, 1991), 37–50; Laurel Thatcher Ulrich, "Wheels, Looms, and the Gender Division of Labor in Eighteenth-Century New England," *William and Mary Quarterly*, 3rd series, 55, no. 1 (1998): 3–38; Laurel Thatcher Ulrich, *Good Wives: Image and Reality in the Lives of Women in Northern New England, 1650–1750* (New York: Vintage Books, 1980), 12–24; and Laurel Thatcher Ulrich, *A Midwife's Tale: The Life of Martha Ballard, Based on Her Diary, 1785–1812* (New York: Vintage Books, 1990). Mary Prentice, *American Register* [St. Albans, Vt.], 14 September 1826; Phebe Darling, *Vermont Gazette*, 13 January 1796.

24. Stacey Helmbrecht-Wilson, *"Went a Shopping": Elite and Middling Women as Consumers in Massachusetts, 1790–1830* (Ph.D. diss., Boston University, 1999), 91, 92, 98–99. Helmbrecht-Wilson was able to trace the sex of purchasers at John Lincoln's store because, unlike most other merchants and shopkeepers, Lincoln recorded in his account books the name of each individual who made a purchase.

25. *Aaron Buckland & John Buckland v. Daniel Hill*, Hartford County Court Files, 1808–March 1809, RG3, CSL; Daniel Hill, *Connecticut Courant*, 4 April 1791.

26. Hannah West, *Vermont Journal*, 5 August 1811. Emphasis mine in Hannah West citation. Dolly Dodge, *Columbian Patriot* [Middlebury, Vt.], 12 January 1814; Thankfull Hutchens, *Connecticut Courant*, 27 May 1807. Alan Taylor, "The Gendered Order of a Rural Village in the Early American Republic" (unpublished essay), has found that women in Otsego County, New York, who printed desertion notices also claimed to own the objects they produced or used in their household labors. In "Provisions for Daughters: The Accounts of Samuel Lane," *House and Home*, Annual Proceedings of the Dublin Seminar for New England Folklife, 1988, ed. Peter Benes (Boston: Boston University Press, 1990), 11–27, Jane C. Nylander analyzes how an eighteenth-century New Hampshire family equipped its daughters for marriage. Samuel Lane gave each of his five daughters beds, bedding, linens, furniture, and kitchen utensils to bring to their marriages, exactly the type of property female desertion notice authors claimed as their own. Similarly, Barbara Ward McLean, "Women's Property and Family

Continuity in Eighteenth-Century Connecticut," *Early American Probate Inventories,* Annual Proceedings of the Dublin Seminar for New England Folklife, 1987, ed. Peter Benes (Boston: Boston University Press, 1989), 74–85, investigates the types of property awarded to unmarried daughters in probated estates. She discovered that these women received "all the items needed to furnish a modest home—including beds, linens, tables, chairs, chests, and a wide variety of housewares."

27. Osterud, *Bonds of Community;* quotation, 2.

28. Boydston, *Home and Work,* 116–19, 153–59. Jedidiah Dudley, *Connecticut Courant,* 24 September 1822; Peter Tatro, *Enterprise and Vermonter* [Vergennes, Vt.], 16 December 1824; Thomas Lewis, *Connecticut Courant,* 16 July 1798; Joseph Sanborn, *Vermont Journal,* 15 July 1811.

29. Norma Basch, *In the Eyes of the Law: Women, Marriage, and Property in Nineteenth-Century New York* (Ithaca, N.Y.: Cornell University Press, 1982), 26–27; Linda K. Kerber, *Women of the Republic: Intellect and Ideology in Revolutionary America* (Chapel Hill: University of North Carolina Press, 1980), 139–55; Marylynn Salmon, *Women and the Law of Property in Early America* (Chapel Hill: University of North Carolina Press, 1986); *Mary Smith v. Marshal Smith,* VSCR, Chittenden County, January 1813, VSL, microfilm.

30. Salmon, *Women and the Law of Property,* esp. 3–14, addresses the tremendous variability in early American interpretations of the common law.

31. *Rachel Nichols v. Joseph Nichols,* VSCR, Chittenden County, January 1805; *Betsey Downer v. John Downer,* VSCR, Chittenden County, July 1821; *Abigail Niles v. William Niles,* VSCR, Chittenden County, December 1814, VSL, microfilm.

32. In four cases the Vermont court awarded land without evidence of children or of the wife's previous ownership of land. One of these women did not have surviving minor children at the time of the divorce and does not appear to have brought property into the marriage. It is likely that the other three women did have children and that this fact was not recorded. In fact, their divorce petitions indicate that these women had lived with their husbands for at least thirteen years, making it extremely likely that they did have children. For a more in-depth discussion of alimony awards, see chapter 6.

33. *Nancy Page v. Benjamin Page,* VSCR, Windsor County, August 1810, VSL, microfilm.

34. Royall Tyler, *Reports of Cases Argued and Determined in the Supreme Court of Judicature of the State of Vermont,* 2 vols. (New York, 1809), 1:409, 1:414.

35. Basch, *In the Eyes of the Law,* 94, and Norma Basch, "Relief in the Premises: Divorce as a Woman's Remedy in New York and Indiana, 1815–1870," *Law and History Review* 8, no. 1 (1990): 9–10, discuss the New York statute. Zephaniah Swift, *Digest of the Laws of the State of Connecticut,* 2 vols.

(New Haven, Conn., 1822), 1:25; Kerber, *Women of the Republic,* 170, 174 discusses the Connecticut statute and practice. The six cases in which the Vermont Supreme Court awarded alimony to women appearing as defendants were *Hezekiah Thompson v. Mary Thompson,* VSCR, Windsor County, August 1803; *Obadiah Hyde v. Clarissa Hyde,* VSCR, Chittenden County, January 1808; *Isaac Rowland v. Lydia Rowland,* VSCR, Windsor County, August 1811; *Sylvester Day v. Avis Day,* VSCR, Chittenden County, January 1814; *Joseph Brown v. Sally Brown,* VSCR, Washington County, September 1823; *Stephen Hollister v. Sarah Hollister,* VSCR, Chittenden County, January 1825, VSL, microfilm.

36. Barbara B. Ferris and Grace Louise Knox, compilers, *Connecticut Divorces: Superior Court Records for the Counties of Litchfield, 1752–1922, and Hartford, 1740–1849* (Bowie, Md.: Heritage Books, 1989), 11–31; Kerber, *Women of the Republic,* 170, 174, found that eighteenth-century Connecticut divorce settlements rarely included any property distribution. *The Public Statute Laws of the State of Connecticut, As Revised and Enacted by the General Assembly, in May 1821* (Hartford, Conn., 1821), 179.

37. *Horace Bissell v. Elizabeth Bissell,* HCDR, February 1823, CSL, microfilm; East Windsor District Probate Records, 1782–1880, No. 529, 2990, NEHGS, microfilm.

38. *Elizabeth Johnson v. Chandler Johnson,* HCDR, November 1804, CSL, microfilm; Farmington District Probate Records, 1769–1880, No. 1782, NEHGS, microfilm; United States Fourth Census, 1820, Connecticut.

39. CALD, 1789–1820, CSL, microfilm. See chapter 6 for a more in-depth discussion of alimony awards.

40. *Kinsman, Executor of Robert Kinsman, v. Kinsman* in Jesse Root, *Reports of Cases Adjudged in the Superior Court and Supreme Court of Errors from July, A.D. 1789, to June, A.D. 1793,* 2 vols. (Hartford: State of Connecticut, 1962), 1:180.

41. Salmon, *Women and the Law of Property,* 125–26.

42. *Nehemiah Dibble v. Mary Hutton,* Connecticut Supreme Court of Errors, Reasons of the Court, June 1803–June 1807, Vol. 97, 5–8, RG 3, State Archives, CSL.

43. Divorces *a mensa et thoro* were legal separations that required husbands to continue supporting their wives and that did not allow the parties to remarry. *Elizabeth May Fitch v. Jehu Brainerd, Esq.,* in Thomas Day, *Reports of Cases Argued and Determined in the Supreme Court of Errors of the State of Connecticut, in the Years 1805, 1806, and 1807,* 5 vols. (Waterbury, Conn., 1898), 2:173.

NOTES TO CHAPTER 4

1. John Bolton, *North Star* [Danville, Vt.], 26 November 1803.

2. Nancy F. Cott, "Eighteenth-Century Family and Social Life Revealed in

Massachusetts Divorce Records," in Nancy F. Cott and Elizabeth H. Pleck, eds., *A Heritage of Her Own: Towards a New Social History of American Women* (New York: Simon and Schuster, 1979), 107–35; Hendrik Hartog, "Marital Exits and Marital Expectations in Nineteenth-Century America," *Georgetown Law Review* 80 (October 1991): 126–29.

3. William Wheeler, *Weekly Wanderer* [Randolph, Vt.], 18 November 1805; Timothy Harris, *Connecticut Courant* [Hartford, Conn.], 1 May 1826; Joseph Root, *Connecticut Courant*, 28 February 1791; Parker Chapy, *Vermont Journal* [Windsor, Vt.], 5 January 1818.

4. Moses Bailey, *Vermont Journal*, 15 December 1794.

5. John Smith, *Watchman* [Montpelier, Vt.], 31 October 1815.

6. Ruth Austin, *Impartial Herald* [Suffield, Conn.], 13 November 1798; "C.," *Impartial Herald*, 13 November 1798.

7. William Blackstone, *Commentaries on the Laws of England*, 2 vols. (1765–1769, rpt. New York, 1836), 1:155, links wives' elopements with adultery; James Kent, *Commentaries on American Law*, 4 vols. (1826, rpt. Boston, 1884), 1:185, also addresses the connections between elopement and adultery; John Severans, *Watchman*, 14 July 1814; Herba Child, *Vermont Republican* [Windsor, Vt.], 3 April 1815; Homes Greenwood, *Connecticut Courant*, 15 April 1799; Moses Allard, *Vermont Journal*, 13 April 1812; Robert Dickey, *Vermont Journal*, 14 December 1802; Parson Greenwood, *American Mercury* [Hartford, Conn.], 3 September 1801; William Andrews, *American Mercury*, 26 August 1802.

8. George Cunningham, *Rutland* [Vt.] *Herald*, 22 April 1799; Ezekial Porter, *Rutland Herald*, 13 May 1799.

9. Fourteen percent of Vermont wives complained of their husbands' sexual misconduct, while 53 percent accused their husbands of failing to provide economic support. Likewise, 20 percent of Connecticut wives accused their husbands of adultery and 67 percent claimed that their husbands had neglected to support them economically.

10. Thankful Hutchens, *Connecticut Courant*, 27 May 1807; Mehitabel Tylor, *Vermont Journal*, 16 February 1802; Lois Vaughan, *Vermont Journal*, 26 August 1796.

11. For a discussion of systems of poor relief in the early national period, see Mimi Abramovitz, *Regulating the Lives of Women: Social Welfare Policy from Colonial Times to the Present* (Boston: South End Press, 1996).

12. Lucy Thayer, *Watchman*, 14 June 1825; Polly Ann Bulkly, *Enterprise and Vermonter* [Vergennes, Vt.], 6 January 1825; Clarissa Post, *American Mercury*, 8 October 1816.

13. Esther Woodbury, *North Star*, 24 June 1809; Sally Meigs, *Rutland Herald*, 5 December 1796; Hester Smith, *Connecticut Courant*, 5 January 1813.

14. John Mack Faragher, *Women and Men on the Overland Trail* (New

Haven, Conn.: Yale University Press, 1979), 110–43, argues that nineteenth-century farm women were isolated from public life and constructed their social circles primarily among family members. Cornelia Hughes Dayton, *Women before the Bar: Gender, Law, and Society in Connecticut, 1639–1789* (Chapel Hill: University of North Carolina Press, 1995), 319–20, 323–24, argues that women were less likely than men to confront any adversary publicly because they could protect their reputations within their smaller social circles without doing so.

15. Jeremiah Richardson, *Vermont Republican*, 28 October 1811; Titus Burr, *American Mercury*, 11 August 1829; James Bacon, *Connecticut Courant*, 12 May 1818; Rueben Hosmer, *Vermont Journal*, 7 August 1807.

16. Isaac Danforth, *Woodstock* [Vt.] *Observer*, 18 July 1820, 19 September 1820; Susan Danforth, *Woodstock Observer*, 8 August 1820; Aaron Colton, *Times* [Hartford, Conn.], 30 September 1817.

17. James Pell, *Green Mountain Patriot* [Peacham, Vt.], 25 June 1805; Abigail Pell, *Green Mountain Patriot*, 9 July 1805, 20 August 1805; Rebecca Read, *Vermont Journal*, 19 May 1790; Belinda Smalley, *Vermont Centinel* [Burlington, Vt.], 2 January 1812.

18. Isaac Case, *Connecticut Courant*, 30 March 1801; Ebenezer Couch, *Connecticut Courant*, 18 May 1801; Joseph Steel, *Connecticut Courant*, 22 February 1804; Benjamin Griffis, *World* [Brattleboro, Vt.], 9 January 1809, 16 January 1809; Mercy Griffis, *World*, 13 February 1809.

19. Ruth Austin, *Impartial Herald*, 13 November 1798.

20. Joan R. Gundersen, "Independence, Citizenship, and the American Revolution," *Signs* 13, no. 1 (1987): 59–77; Jan Lewis, "The Republican Wife: Virtue and Seduction in the Early Republic," *William and Mary Quarterly*, 3rd series, 44, no. 4 (1987): 689–721; Nancy Isenberg, *Sex and Citizenship in Antebellum America* (Chapel Hill: University of North Carolina Press, 1998), esp. chapter 2; Ruth Austin, *Impartial Herald*, 13 November 1798.

21. Abigail Pell, *Green Mountain Patriot*, 20 August 1805; Belinda Smalley, *Vermont Centinel*, 2 January 1812.

22. Jacob Lindsly, *American Mercury*, 3 October 1796; Bristol, Connecticut, Deeds, Vol. 8, 131, 462, CSL, microfilm; Farmington District Probate Records, 1769–1800, No. 1824, NEHGS, microfilm.

23. On warning out, see Ruth Wallis Herndon, *Unwelcome Americans: Living on the Margin in Early New England* (Philadelphia: University of Pennsylvania Press, 2001), 1–21; Luke Graham, *Reporter* [Brattleboro, Vt.], 8 July 1809; Dummerston, Vermont, Town Proceedings, 3 June 1809, 18 July 1809, GSCSV, microfilm. Zadock Thompson, *A Gazetteer of the State of Vermont* (Montpelier, Vt., 1824), 219–20; *Elisha Hutchinson v. The Inhabitants of Pomfret, Benjamin Brown & Henry Sweetser v. Elisha Hutchinson, William Allen v. Elisha Hutchinson*, WCCR, September 1797, Vol. 4, 99, 235, BHL, microfilm; Pomfret, Vermont, Land Records, Vol. 3, 29, GSCSV, microfilm.

24. Elisha Hutchinson, *Vermont Journal*, 13 October 1797; Jerusha Hutchinson, *Vermont Journal*, 17 October 1797; VRSV, 1760–1870, GSCSV, microfilm.

25. *Vermont Journal*, 10 November 1797.

26. Isaac Danforth, *Woodstock Observer*, 18 July 1820; Susan Danforth, *Woodstock Observer*, 8 August 1820.

27. Isaac Danforth, *Woodstock Observer*, 19 September 1820.

28. Isaac Danforth, *Woodstock Observer*, 19 September 1820; lists of local justices of the peace are found in *Journal of the General Assembly of the State of Vermont, 1814* (Windsor, Vt. 1814); *Journal of the General Assembly of the State of Vermont, 1815* (Windsor, Vt., 1815); *Journal of the General Assembly of the State of Vermont, 1816* (Rutland, Vt., 1816). United States Third Census, 1810; United States Fourth Census, 1820; United States Fifth Census, 1830; Gardner Winslow, *Woodstock Observer*, 10 October 1820.

29. Susan Danforth, Gardner Winslow, *Woodstock Observer*, 10 October 1820. That Susan Danforth and Gardner Winslow intended their postings to protect Susan's supporters from the threat of legal action by Isaac Danforth is likely. Thanks to Hendrik Hartog for this insight.

30. Isaac Danforth, *Woodstock Observer*, 24 October 1820.

31. *Danforth v. Briggs*, WCCR, December 1820, Vol. 13, 139, Vol. 4, 320, BHL, microfilm; *Danforth v. Briggs*, VSCR, Windsor County, August 1821, VSL, microfilm; Hartford District Probate Court Records, Vol. 9, 423, GSCSV, microfilm; VRSV, 1760–1870, GSCSV, microfilm.

32. Tapping Reeve, *The Law of Baron and Femme, of Parent and Child, Guardian and Ward, Master and Servant, and of the Powers of the Courts of Chancery* (1816, rpt. Albany, N.Y., 1862), 139, 142.

NOTES TO CHAPTER 5

1. David Read, *Vermont Journal* [Windsor, Vt.], 28 April 1790; Rebecca Read, *Vermont Journal*, 19 May 1790; "Journal of James Whitelaw, 1773–1793," MS, Vermont Historical Society, Montpelier, Vt.; Abby Maria Hemenway, ed., *The Vermont Historical Gazetteer*, 5 vols. (Burlington, Vt., 1867) 1:376; John E. Goodrich, ed., *The State of Vermont Rolls of the Soldiers in the Revolutionary War, 1775 to 1783* (Rutland, Vt.: Tuttle, 1904), 53; Ryegate, Vermont, Deeds, Vol. 1, 91–92, GSCSV, microfilm; Ryegate, Vermont, Town Records, Vol. 1, 6, GSCSV, microfilm; Caledonia District Probate Court Records, Vol. 7, 542–43, Vol. 8, 355–59, GSCSV, microfilm; VRSV, 1760–1870, GSCSV, microfilm.

2. No record exists of a divorce; however, it is possible that the couple did divorce, as no mention is made of David as Rebecca's husband in the probate records concerning her estate.

3. *Barbour Index to the Vital Records of the State of Connecticut,* NEHGS, microfilm; John Smith, *Connecticut Courant* [Hartford, Conn.], 22 December 1812; Hester Smith, *Connecticut Courant* [Hartford, Conn.], 5 January 1813; Farmington District Probate Records, 1769–1880, NEHGS, microfilm.

4. I determined that a couple had reconciled if the husband posted a newspaper notice announcing the reconciliation, if the couple registered the birth of a child more than nine months after the appearance of the initial elopement notice, if the husband mentioned his wife in his will, or if the probate court set aside dower for the wife when the husband had died intestate. I determined that a couple had permanently separated with no evidence of divorce if, after an elopement, neither spouse petitioned for a divorce, but the husband and wife appeared separately on census or tax records, the wife appeared in court in her own name, or the wife left a will or had an estate in probate before the husband died. It is likely that some of these couples did divorce, but the records have not survived.

5. These percentages are for couples with known outcomes only.

6. William McIntash, *Vermont Journal,* 30 August 1803; Freelove McIntash, *Vermont Journal,* 4 October 1803; VRSV, 1760–1870, GSCSV, microfilm; Wyman Ainsworth, *Weekly Wanderer* [Randolph, Vt.], 28 March 1801; VRSV, 1760–1870, GSCSV, microfilm.

7. The outcome for the eighth Vermont wife who brought property into her marriage is unknown. Of the four remaining Connecticut wives who brought real estate into their marriages, three reconciled. The outcome for the fourth is unknown.

8. Woodstock, Vermont, Land Records, Vol. 7, 455, GSCSV, microfilm; VRSV, 1760–1870, GSCSV, microfilm; United States Fourth Census, 1820, Vermont; Abel Paine, *Woodstock* [Vt.] *Observer,* 11 April 1820; Thomas Hutchens, *Connecticut Courant,* 20 May 1807; Thankful Hutchens, *Connecticut Courant,* 27 May 1807; East Windsor District Probate Court Records, 1782–1880, NEHGS, microfilm.

9. Esther Woodbury, *North Star* [Danville, Vt.], 24 June 1809; Ranna Cossit, *Connecticut Courant,* 7 October 1807; Job Tylor, *Vermont Journal,* 9 March 1802; VRSV, 1760–1870, GSCSV, microfilm.

10. Salmon Cogswell, *Connecticut Courant,* 6 October 1794, 3 November 1794; Elam Pease, *Connecticut Courant,* 9 March 1819; Abigail Pease, *Connecticut Courant,* 16 March 1819; East Windsor Deeds, Vol. 21, 26, CSL, microfilm.

11. Amos Sanderson, *Vermont Republican* [Windsor, Vt.], 6 June 1814; Springfield, Vermont, Land Records, Vol. 5, 327, 328, 476, 478; 6, 139, 140; 7, 10, GSCSV, microfilm; United States Fourth Census, 1820, Vermont; VRSV, 1760–1870, GSCSV, microfilm; Aaron Colton, *Times* [Hartford, Conn.], 16

September 1817, 30 September 1817; United States Fourth Census, 1820, Connecticut; Hartford County Superior Court Records, 1817–1821, RG 3, CSL; Hartford County Court Defaults, Vol. 41, 1818–1820; Vol. 43, 1823–1830, RG3, CSL; Hartford County Court Records, Vol. 23, August 1819–April 1828, RG3, CSL; *The Pocket Register for the City of Hartford* (Hartford, Conn., 1825), CSL, microfilm.

12. A number of scholars discuss such informal separations and remarriages. Nancy F. Cott, *Public Vows: A History of Marriage and the Nation* (Cambridge: Harvard University Press, 2000), 30–40; Michael Grossberg, *Governing the Hearth: Law and the Family in Nineteenth-Century America* (Chapel Hill: University of North Carolina Press), chapters 3 and 4; Carole Shammas, *A History of Household Government in America* (Charlottesville: University of Virginia Press, 2002), 99–107, point out the acceptance of informal, or irregular, marriages in the early United States. Courts and communities routinely considered couples who had lived together openly as husband and wife to be married. Given this social and legal milieu, informal "divorce" also was possible and, in some cases, deemed acceptable by local communities. Beverly Schwartzberg, " 'Lots of Them Did That': Desertion, Bigamy, and Marital Fluidity in Late-Nineteenth-Century America," *Journal of Social History* 37, no. 3 (2004): 573–600, chronicles a rich assortment of informal marriages, separations, and remarriages in the middle to late nineteenth century.

13. Anna Norris, *North Star,* 25 July 1817.

14. Stephen Kimball, *National Standard* [Middlebury, Vt.], 11 December 1821; Esther Kimball, *National Standard,* 18 December 1821; VRSV, 1760–1870, GSCSV, microfilm. Records indicate that other wives in the sample population applied for poor relief; however, there is no evidence that they received it. See Mary Beth Sievens, " 'The Wicked Agency of Others': Community, Law, and Marital Conflict in Early National Vermont," *Journal of the Early Republic* 21, no. 1 (2001): 25–28, and the discussion of Susan Danforth in chapter 4.

15. Uriah Hayes, *Vermont Republican,* 11 October 1813; Hugh Montgomery, *Vergennes* [Vt.] *Gazette,* 26 March 1801; Polly Montgomery, *Vergennes Gazette,* 14 May 1801.

16. Fanny Baker, *Vergennes Gazette,* 8 November 1798.

17. Joan R. Gundersen and Gwen Victor Gampel, "Married Women's Legal Status in Eighteenth-Century New York and Virginia," *William and Mary Quarterly,* 3rd series, 39 (January 1982): 131–33; Linda K. Kerber, *Women of the Republic: Intellect and Ideology in Revolutionary America* (Chapel Hill: University of North Carolina Press, 1980), 148–52. For an analysis of women legitimately acting as *femes sole,* see Lisa Wilson Waciega, *Life after Death: Widows in Pennsylvania, 1750–1850* (Philadelphia: Temple University Press, 1992).

18. See chapter 2 for a more in-depth discussion of this case.

19. Asa Aikens, *Reports of Cases Argued and Determined in the Supreme Court of the State of Vermont*, 2 vols. (Windsor, Vt., 1827), 1:174–79; James Kent, *Commentaries on American Law*, 4 vols. (1826, rpt. Boston, 1884), 2:185.

20. Titus Thomas, *American Mercury* [Hartford, Conn.], 28 May 1807; Hartford Deeds, Vol. 29, 64, 68; Vol. 32, 135, CSL, microfilm.

21. VRSV, 1760–1870, GSCSV, microfilm; Kenelm Winslow, *Woodstock Observer*, 16 October 1821; Bridgewater, Vermont, Land Records, Vol. 3, 50, 132, 133, GSCSV, microfilm; Bridgewater, Vermont, Grand List for 1830, Vermont Historical Society, Montpelier, Vt.

22. WCCR, Vol. 13, 226, BHL, microfilm.

23. Other couples, such as Titus and Julia Thomas, did not announce a mutual separation, but their actions after the separation indicate that both parties had agreed to live apart.

24. Hendrik Hartog, "Marital Exits and Marital Expectations in Nineteenth-Century America," *Georgetown Law Journal* 80, no. 1 (1991): 95–129; Thomas Brigham, *Washingtonian* [Windsor, Vt.], 17 December 1810; Levi Ball, *North Star*, 17 January 1820; Ebenezer Couch, *Connecticut Courant*, 21 March 1804.

25. Frederick W. Richardson, *Eighteenth-Century Springfield: From Wilderness to Vermont Statehood, 1751–1791* (Newport, N.H.: F. W. Richardson, 1991), 152, 155, 156, 165; Henry Closson, "History of Springfield, Vermont to 1870," 46–47, MS, Vermont Historical Society, Montpelier, Vt.; Mary Eva Baker, *Folklore of Springfield* (Springfield, Vt.: [The Altrurian Club of Springfield, Vt.], 1922), 87; Moses Gaylord, *Vermont Journal*, 9 March 1795.

26. United States Second Census, 1800, Vermont; United States Third Census, 1810, Vermont; Springfield, Vermont, Land Records, Vol. 2, 507, 508; 3, 718, 719, GSCSV, microfilm; WCCR, Vol. 5, 91; 7, 66; 10, 343, 344, BHL, microfilm; VRSV, 1760–1870, GSCSV, microfilm; WDPCR, Vol. 14, 589–91, GSCSV, microfilm.

27. WDPCR, Vol. 14, 589, GSCSV, microfilm; Springfield, Vermont, Town Records, Vol. 3, 372, GSCSV, microfilm; William Slade, ed., *The Laws of Vermont, of a Publick and Permanent Nature: Coming Down to and including, the Year 1824* (Windsor, Vt., 1825), 351–52.

28. WDPCR, Vol. 14, 589–91, GSCSV, microfilm.

29. WDPCR, Vol. 14, 225–27, 370, 589–91, GSCSV, microfilm. Moses Gaylord's claim to Margaret's real estate is unclear because it is difficult to determine how Margaret got this property. Approximately forty acres of the real estate was Margaret's dower, the use of which she received upon the death of her first husband. Moses would have had no claim to this property. Margaret's son, William, had inherited eighty acres from her first husband; however, when William died in 1827, he possessed only thirty acres of real estate, which was sold to pay his debts. If Margaret had purchased her remaining real estate during her legal marriage to Moses, he would have been the lawful owner of that property. However,

Springfield land records do not record any land purchased by Margaret or Moses. WDPCR, Vol. 2, 8–15; 11, 120–23, GSCSV, microfilm.

30. Joseph Ayres, *Washingtonian*, 6 June 1814.

NOTES TO CHAPTER 6

1. *Eunice Snow v. Daniel Snow,* VSCR, Windsor County, January 1818, VSL, microfilm; WDPCR, Vol. 11, 452–55, GSCSV, microfilm.

2. WDPCR, Vol. 16, 481–82, GSCSV, microfilm.

3. For a comprehensive overview of the evolution of divorce law and practice in the Western world, see Roderick Phillips, *Putting Asunder: A History of Divorce in Western Society* (Cambridge: Cambridge University Press, 1988). Nancy F. Cott, "Divorce and the Changing Status of Women in Eighteenth-Century Massachusetts," *William and Mary Quarterly,* 3rd series, 33, no. 4 (1976): 586–614; Carl N. Degler, *At Odds: Women and the Family in America from the Revolution to the Present* (New York: Oxford University Press, 1980), 16–17; Glenda Riley, *Divorce: An American Tradition* (New York: Oxford University Press, 1991); Joan R. Gundersen, "Independence, Citizenship, and the American Revolution," *Signs* 13, no. 1 (1987): 73; Linda K. Kerber, *Women of the Republic: Intellect and Ideology in Revolutionary America* (Chapel Hill: University of North Carolina Press, 1980), 159–84; Norma Basch, "Relief in the Premises: Divorce as a Woman's Remedy in New York and Indiana, 1815–1870," *Law and History Review* 8, no. 1 (1990): 1–24; Norma Basch, *Framing American Divorce: From the Revolutionary Generation to the Victorians* (Berkeley: University of California Press, 1999), 99–120.

4. Records indicate that only one Connecticut man in the sample population remarried after his divorce. In all likelihood, these numbers underrepresent the number of divorced women who remarried, as some may have moved to other states before remarrying. Nevertheless, these extremely low numbers are striking.

5. Petition of Temperance Hill, CALD, 1, 75, CSL, microfilm; *Anne Kittredge v. Timothy Kittredge,* VSCR, Windsor County, October 1799, VSL, microfilm; Petition of Abigail Bedient, CALD, 1, 19, CSL, microfilm.

6. *Sabrina Cooley v. Royal Cooley,* VSCR, Chittenden County, January 1828, VSL, microfilm.

7. *Anna Chamberlin v. Asa Chamberlin,* VSCR, Chittenden County, January 1807, VSL, microfilm; Petition of Jemima Sill, CALD, 2, 35, CSL, microfilm.

8. Of the ten women who petitioned the assembly for both divorce and custody, three were denied divorces. The other seven received divorces and custody. Men petitioned for divorce on the grounds that their wives had committed adultery and had borne children as a result of their illicit unions.

9. Sarah Hall, *American Mercury* [Hartford, Conn.], 23 December 1802;

Sarah Hall v. Isaac Hall, Litchfield County Divorce Records, September 1811, CSL, microfilm; *Harriot Allen v. Rufus Allen*, VSCR, Chittenden County, January 1812, VSL, microfilm.

10. John and Abigail Rice, *Vermont Journal* [Windsor, Vt.], 19 July 1813; *Abigail Rice v. John Rice*, VSCR, Windsor County, January 1817, VSL, microfilm; Hartland, Vermont, Land Records, Vol. 8, 222; 10, 161, GSCSV, microfilm; WCCR, Vol. 12, 141, 251, BHL, microfilm.

11. Amasa Moor, *American Mercury*, 7 November 1799; Hartford County Connecticut Superior Court Records, 1804–1810, February 1807, RG 3, CSL; Connecticut Land Records, Granby Deeds, Vol. 6, 460–61, CSL, microfilm; Hartford County Court Files, December 1804–March 1805, Box 300, RG 3, CSL; Hartford County Court Defaults, Vol. 35, 1804–1808, RG 3, CSL.

12. Dwight quoted in Benjamin Trumball, *"What Therefore God Hath Joined Together, Let Not Man Put Asunder": An Appeal to the Public, with Respect to the Unlawfulness of Divorces* (New Haven, Conn., 1819), 38. Emphasis appears in Trumball.

13. Clarence Winthrop Bowen, *The History of Woodstock, Connecticut, Genealogies of Woodstock Families*, 8 vols. (Worcester: American Antiquarian Society, 1943), 8:262; VRSV, 1760–1870, GSCSV, microfilm; Hartford District Probate Records, Vol. 2, 364; 3, 61, 203; 4, 170, GSCSV, microfilm; *Mary Watkins v. John Watkins*, VSCR, Windsor County, August 1811, VSL, microfilm.

14. Hartford District Probate Court Records, Vol. 4, 452, 515, 516; 6, 12, GSCSV, microfilm. For Vermont law on intestacy, see William Slade, ed., *The Laws of Vermont, of a Publick and Permanent Nature: Coming Down to and including, the Year 1824* (Windsor, Vt., 1825), 347.

15. Sixty-five percent of Connecticut alimony grants contained cash awards; 41 percent of Vermont alimony awards included cash.

16. If husbands owned property within the jurisdiction of the court, the court could order the seizure and sale of the property to satisfy the cash award. Elias Hall, *A Disclosure of Facts, in Consequence of a Decree for Alimony by the Supreme Court, Addison County, January Term, 1823, against Elias Hall* (Montpelier, Vt., 1825); *Rachel Hayes v. Uriah Hayes*, VSCR, Windsor County, February 1819, VSL, microfilm; *Rachel Hayes v. Uriah Hayes*, WCCR, Vol. 13, 414, BHL, microfilm.

17. *Betsey Rice v. Rufus Rice*, VSCR, Windsor County, August 1813, VSL, microfilm; *Marcia Belden v. John Belden*, VSCR, Windsor County, August 1809, VSL, microfilm; *Harriot Allen v. Rufus Allen*, VSCR, Chittenden County, January 1812, VSL, microfilm.

18. *Deborah Scott v. John S. Scott*, VSCR, Windsor County, June 1825, VSL, microfilm; William Monroe Newton, *History of Barnard, Vermont, with Family Genealogies, 1761–1927*, 2 vols. (Montpelier: Vermont Historical Society, 1928), 2:461.

19. *Abigail Rice v. John Rice,* VSCR, Windsor County, January 1817, VSL, microfilm; *Elizabeth Tilden v. Stephen Tilden,* VSCR, Windsor County, August 1803, VSL, microfilm; Reading, Vermont, Deeds, Vol. 8, 296, GSCSV, microfilm.

20. In seven cases in which the courts and assembly awarded divorced women land that the women had not possessed before their marriages as alimony, the records do not mention children; however, in five of these cases, the couples had been married for at least eight years before divorcing, making it likely that the women did have children for whom they needed to provide.

21. *Polly Dustin v. Stephen Dustin,* VSCR, Windsor County, August 1810, VSL, microfilm; Resolve granting a divorce to Abigail Bedient, CALD, 1, 20, CSL, microfilm; Resolve granting a divorce to Clarissa Shepard, CALD, 2, 34, CSL; Resolve granting a divorce to Jemima Sill, CALD, 2, 36, CSL, microfilm.

22. *Lois Hubbard v. Watts Hubbard,* VSCR, Windsor County, August 1811, VSL, microfilm; Fourth United States Census, 1820, Vermont; WDPCR, Vol. 15, 498; 20, 116, 120, GSCSV, microfilm.

NOTES TO THE AFTERWORD

1. Stephen Hiscock, *Connecticut Courant* [Hartford, Conn.], 22 December 1800.

2. Benjamin Norris, *North Star* [Danville, Vt.], 28 October 1809; 2 December 1809.

3. For a discussion of the development of ideals of domestic privacy, see Nancy F. Cott, *The Bonds of Womanhood: "Woman's Sphere" in New England, 1780–1835* (New Haven, Conn.: Yale University Press, 1977); Steven Mintz and Susan Kellogg, *Domestic Revolutions: A Social History of American Family Life* (New York: Free Press, 1988); Mary P. Ryan, *Cradle of the Middle Class: The Family in Oneida County, New York, 1790–1865* (Cambridge: Cambridge University Press, 1981); and Barbara Welter, "The Cult of True Womanhood: 1820–1860," *American Quarterly* 18, no. 2 (1966): 151–74. See Linda K. Kerber, "Separate Spheres, Female Worlds, Woman's Place: The Rhetoric of Woman's History," *Journal of American History* 75, no. 1 (1988): 9–39, for a review of the historiography of separate spheres.

4. John Woodruff, *North Star,* 10 June 1809.

Select Bibliography

MANUSCRIPT SOURCES

American Antiquarian Society, Worcester, Mass.
Eastman, Charles G. (1816–1860). "A Picture." Vermont Broadsides.
Bailey-Howe Library, University of Vermont, Burlington, Vt.
Windsor County Court Records, 1789–1825. Microfilm.
Connecticut State Library, Hartford, Conn.
Bristol, Connecticut, Deeds. Microfilm.
Connecticut Archives Lotteries and Divorces, Second Series, 1789–1820. Microfilm.
Connecticut Archives, Series 2, Insolvent Debtors, 1750–1820. Microfilm.
Connecticut Supreme Court of Errors, Reasons of the Court, June 1803–June 1807, Record Group 3.
East Windsor, Connecticut, Deeds. Microfilm.
Granby, Connecticut, Deeds. Microfilm.
Hartford, Connecticut, Deeds. Microfilm.
Hartford County, County Court Defaults, 1775–1855, Record Group 3.
Hartford County, County Court Files, 1713–1855, Record Group 3.
Hartford County, County Court Records, 1666–1881, Record Group 3.
Hartford County Court Divorce Records, 1740–1849. Microfilm.
Hartford County Superior Court Records, 1798–1827, Record Group 3.
Litchfield County Divorce Records, 1752–1922. Microfilm.
General Services Center of the State of Vermont, Middlesex, Vt.
Bridgewater, Vermont, Land Records. Microfilm.
Caledonia District Probate Court Records. Microfilm.
Dummerston, Vermont, Town Proceedings, 1809. Microfilm.
Hartford District Probate Court Records. Microfilm.
Hartland, Vermont, Land Records. Microfilm.
Pomfret, Vermont, Land Records. Microfilm.
Reading, Vermont, Deeds. Microfilm.
Royalton, Vermont, Deeds. Microfilm.
Ryegate, Vermont, Deeds. Microfilm.

Ryegate, Vermont, Town Records. Microfilm.
Springfield, Vermont, Land Records. Microfilm.
Springfield, Vermont, Town Records. Microfilm.
Vital Records of the State of Vermont, 1760–1870. Microfilm.
Windsor District Probate Court Records. Microfilm.
Windsor Superior Court Civil Case Judgments, 1813–1814.
Woodstock, Vermont, Land Records. Microfilm.
New England Historic Genealogical Society, Boston, Mass.
Barbour Index to the Vital Records of the State of Connecticut. Microfilm.
East Windsor District [Conn.] Probate Court Records, 1782–1880. Microfilm.
Farmington District [Conn.] Probate Court Records, 1769–1880. Microfilm.
Windsor District [Conn.] Probate Court Records, 1782–1880. Microfilm.
Vermont Historical Society
Bridgewater, Vermont, Grand List, 1830.
Closson, Henry. "History of Springfield, Vermont to 1870."
Journal of James Whitelaw, 1773–1793.
Vermont State Library
Vermont Supreme Court Records. Chittenden County, January 1800–January
   1834. Microfilm.
Vermont Supreme Court Records. Washington County, September 1821–March
   1829. Microfilm.
Vermont Supreme Court Records. Windsor County, February 1794–June 1825.
   Microfilm.

CONNECTICUT NEWSPAPERS

American Mercury [Hartford], 1784–1830+.
Connecticut Courant [Hartford], 1764–.
Connecticut Intelligencer [Hartford], 1804.
Connecticut Mirror [Hartford], 1809–1820+.
Hartford Gazette, 1794–1795.
Impartial Herald [Suffield], 1797–1799.
New Star [Hartford], 1796.
Times [Hartford], 1817–1820.

VERMONT NEWSPAPERS

Advertiser [St. Albans], 1808.
American Register [Arlington], 1816–1818.
American Repository [St. Albans], 1826+.
American Yeoman [Brattleboro], 1817–1818.
Anti-Masonic Republican [Middlebury], 1829+.

Argus [Putney], 1797–1799.
Champlain Reporter [St. Albans], 1809–1810.
Christian Herald [Middlebury], 1816.
Christian Messenger [Middlebury], 1816–1819.
Columbian Patriot [Middlebury], 1813–1815.
Enterprise and Vermonter [Vergennes], 1824+.
Epitome of the World [Bennington], 1807.
Farmer's Herald [St. Johnsbury], 1828+.
Farmer's Library [Rutland], 1793–1794.
Farmer's Weekly Messenger [Brattleboro], 1823–1830.
Federal Galaxy [Brattleboro], 1797–1803.
Franklin County Advertiser [St. Albans], 1810–1811.
Free Press [Burlington], 1827–.
Freeman's Press [Montpelier], 1809–1812.
Gazette [Burlington], 1814–1817, 1819–1820.
Gazette [Poultney], 1822–1824.
Green Mountain Farmer [Bennington], 1809–1816.
Green Mountain Palladium [Chester], 1807–1808.
Green Mountain Patriot [Peacham], 1798–1807, 1809–1810.
Herald of Vermont [Rutland], 1792.
Independent Freeholder [Brattleboro], 1808–1809.
Mercury [Burlington], 1796–1797.
Mercury [Middlebury], 1801–1810.
Messenger [Brattleboro], 1824–1830.
Mirror [Middlebury], 1812–1816.
Morning Ray [Windsor], 1791–1792.
National Standard [Middlebury], 1815–1820.
News-Letter [Bennington], 1811–1815.
North Star [Danville], 1807–1820+.
Northern Intelligencer [Burlington], 1814.
Northern Memento [Woodstock], 1805–1806.
Northern Spectator [Poultney], 1825–1830.
Orange Nightingale [Newbury], 1796–1797.
Ploughman [Bennington], 1801–1802.
Post-Boy [Windsor], 1805–1807.
Religious Reporter [Middlebury], 1820.
Reporter [Brattleboro], 1803–1820+.
Rutland Herald, 1794–.
Tablet of the Times [Bennington], 1797.
Vergennes Gazette, 1798–1801.
Vermont Advocate [Chelsea], 1828.
Vermont American [Middlebury], 1828–1830.

Vermont Centinel [Burlington], 1801–1820+.
Vermont Courier [Rutland], 1808–1810.
Vermont Gazette [Bennington], 1783–1807.
Vermont Intelligencer [Bellows Falls], 1817–1820+.
Vermont Journal [Windsor], 1783–.
Vermont Luminary [East Randolph], 1829.
Vermont Mercury [Rutland], 1802–1804.
Vermont Patriot [Montpelier], 1826–1830.
Vermont Precursor [Montpelier], 1806–1807.
Vermont Republican [Windsor], 1809–1820+.
Washingtonian [Windsor], 1810–1816.
Watchman [Montpelier], 1807–1820+.
Weekly Wanderer [Randolph], 1800–1810.
Woodstock Observer, 1820+.
World [Bennington], 1807–1809.

OTHER NEWSPAPERS AND MAGAZINES

American Museum [Philadelphia, Pa.], January 1788, July 1788, December 1789.
Gazette [Portsmouth, N.H.], 1790–1830.
Hampshire Gazette [Northampton, Mass.], 1790–1830.
National Recorder [Philadelphia, Pa.], July 31, 1819.
New England Farmer [Boston, Mass.], June 28, 1823.
New York Weekly Magazine [New York, N.Y.], March 22, 1797.
South Carolina Weekly Museum [Charleston, S.C.], May 27, 1797.
The Weekly Visitor; or, Ladies' Miscellany [New York, N.Y.], February 11, 1804.

STATUTES, PUBLISHED COURT DECISIONS,
AND LEGAL TREATISES

Aikens, Asa. *Reports of Cases Argued and Determined in the Supreme Court of the State of Vermont.* 2 vols. Windsor, Vt., 1827.
Blackstone, William. *Commentaries on the Laws of England.* 2 vols. 1765–1769; rpt. New York, 1836.
Day, Thomas. *Reports of Cases Argued and Determined in the Supreme Court of Errors of the State of Connecticut, in the Years 1805, 1806, and 1807.* Rpt. Waterbury, Conn., 1898.
[Jacob, Giles]. *Everyman His Own Lawyer.* New York, 1768.
Journal of the General Assembly of the State of Vermont, 1814. Windsor, Vt., 1814.

Journal of the General Assembly of the State of Vermont, 1815. Windsor, Vt., 1815.

Journal of the General Assembly of the State of Vermont, 1816. Windsor, Vt., 1816.

Kent, James. *Commentaries on American Law.* 4 vols. 1826; rpt. Boston, 1884.

[M'Dougal, John]. *The Farmer's Assistant; or, Every Man His Own Lawyer.* Chillicothe, Oh., 1813.

The Public Statute Laws of the State of Connecticut, As Revised and Enacted by the General Assembly, in May 1821. Hartford, Conn., 1821.

Reeve, Tapping. *The Law of Baron and Feme, of Parent and Child, Guardian and Ward, Master and Servant, and of the Powers of the Courts of Chancery.* 1816; rpt. Albany, N.Y., 1862.

The Revised Statutes of the State of Connecticut. Hartford, Conn., 1849.

Root, Jesse. *Reports of Cases Adjudged in the Superior Court and Supreme Court of Errors.* 2 vols. Rpt. Hartford, Conn., 1962.

Slade, William, ed. *The Laws of Vermont, of a Publick and Permanent Nature: Coming Down to and including, the Year 1824.* Windsor, Vt., 1825.

———. *Vermont State Papers.* Middlebury, Vt., 1823.

Statutes of the State of Vermont. Bennington, Vt., 1791.

Swift, Zephaniah. *Digest of the Laws of the State of Connecticut.* 2 Vols. New Haven, Conn., 1822–1823.

Tyler, Royal. *Reports of Cases Argued and Determined in the Supreme Court of Judicature of the State of Vermont.* 2 vols. New York, 1809–1810.

SERMONS, ADVICE MANUALS, AND OTHER PUBLISHED PRIMARY SOURCES

Andrews, Frank D., ed. *BusinessMen of the City of Hartford (Connecticut) in the Year 1799.* Vineland, N.J.: F. D. Andrews, 1909. Connecticut State Library. Microfilm.

———. *Directory for the City of Hartford for the Year 1799.* Vineland, N.J.: F. D. Andrews, 1910. Connecticut State Library. Microfilm.

[Anon.]. *Advice in Order to Prevent Poverty; to Which Is Added Directions to a Young Tradesman. Written by an Old One.* Windsor, Vt., 1792.

[Anon.]. *The Wife.* Boston, 1806.

Bean, James. *The Christian Minister's Affectionate Advice to a Married Couple.* Boston, 1815.

Burton, Asa. *A Sermon, Preached at the Funeral of Mrs. Joanna Shaw, Consort of Colonel Dan Shaw, of Lime, N.H..* Hanover, N.H., 1804.

Giles, William. *The Guide to Domestic Happiness.* New Haven, Conn., 1804.

Hall, Elias. *A Disclosure of Facts, in Consequence of a Decree for Alimony by the Supreme Court, Addison County, January Term, 1823, against Elias Hall.* Montpelier, Vt., 1825.

Hartford City Directory for 1828. Hartford, Conn., 1828. Connecticut State Library. Microfilm.

James, John Angell. *The Family Monitor; or, A Help to Domestic Happiness.* Boston, 1829.

Jay, William. *The Mutual Duties of Husbands and Wives.* Boston, 1808.

Kenrick, William. *The Whole Duty of Woman.* Windsor, Vt., 1792.

Parker, Isaiah. *A Funeral Discourse, the Substance of Which Was Delivered in Cavendish; at the Interment of Mrs. Esther Chaplin, Wife of Capt. William Chaplin.* Harvard, Mass., 1807.

Peale, Charles W. *An Essay to Promote Domestic Happiness.* Philadelphia, Pa., 1812.

The Pocket Register for the City of Hartford. Hartford, Conn., 1825. Connecticut State Library. Microfilm.

Skinner, Warren. *The Influence of the Female Character. A Sermon on the Importance and Influence of Female Character.* Cavendish, Vt., [182?].

Trumball, Benjamin. *"What Therefore God Hath Joined Together, Let Not Man Put Asunder": An Appeal to the Public, with Respect to the Unlawfulness of Divorces.* New Haven, Conn., 1819.

Tullar, Martin. *A Concise System of Family Duty: Comprising the Relative Duties of Husbands, and Wives.* Windsor, Vt., 1802.

Wright, Chester. *Jesus Weeping at Lazarus's Grave. A Sermon, Preached at Montpelier, Dec. 27, 1813, at the Burial of Mrs. Hannah Loomis.* Montpelier, Vt., 1814.

SECONDARY SOURCES

Abramovitz, Mimi. *Regulating the Lives of Women: Social Welfare Policy from Colonial Times to the Present.* Boston: South End Press, 1996.

Aldrich, Lewis Cass, and Frank R. Holmes, eds. *History of Windsor County Vermont with Illustrations and Biographical Sketches of Some of Its Prominent Men and Pioneers.* Syracuse, N.Y., 1891.

Allen, Ira. *The Natural and Political History of the State of Vermont.* London, 1798.

Baker, Mary Eva. *Folklore of Springfield.* Springfield, Vt.: [The Altrurian Club of Springfield, Vt.], 1922.

Bandel, Betty. "What the Good Laws of Man Hath Put Asunder . . ." *Vermont History* 46, no. 4 (1978): 221–33.

Barron, Hal S. *Those Who Stayed Behind: Rural Society in Nineteenth-Century New England.* Cambridge: Cambridge University Press, 1984.

Basch, Norma. *Framing American Divorce: From the Revolutionary Generation to the Victorians.* Berkeley: University of California Press, 1999.

——. *In the Eyes of the Law: Women, Marriage, and Property in Nineteenth-Century New York.* Ithaca, N.Y.: Cornell University Press, 1982.

——. "Relief in the Premises: Divorce as a Woman's Remedy in New York and Indiana, 1815–1870." *Law and History Review* 8, no. 1 (1990): 1–24.

Bowen, Clarence Winthrop. *The History of Woodstock, Connecticut, Genealogies of Woodstock Families.* 8 vols. Worcester, Mass.: American Antiquarian Society, 1943.

Boydston, Jeanne. *Home and Work: Housework, Wages, and the Ideology of Labor in the Early Republic.* New York: Oxford University Press, 1990.

——. "The Woman Who Wasn't There: Women's Market Labor and the Transition to Capitalism in the United States." *Journal of the Early Republic* 16, no. 2 (1996): 183–206.

Breen, T. H. "Baubles of Britain: The American and Consumer Revolutions of the Eighteenth Century." *Past and Present* 119 (May 1988): 73–104.

——. "An Empire of Goods: The Anglicization of Colonial America, 1690–1776." *Journal of British Studies* 25, no. 4 (1986): 467–99.

Bushman, Richard L. *From Puritan to Yankee: Character and the Social Order in Connecticut, 1690–1765.* Cambridge: Harvard University Press, 1967.

——. *The Refinement of America: Persons, Houses, Cities.* New York: Knopf, 1992.

Censer, Jane Turner. "'Smiling through Her Tears': Ante-Bellum Southern Women and Divorce." *American Journal of Legal History* 25, no. 1 (1981): 24–47.

Chambers-Schiller, Lee Virginia. *Liberty a Better Husband: Single Women in America: The Generations of 1780–1840.* New Haven, Conn.: Yale University Press, 1984.

Clark, Christopher. "Household Economy, Market Exchange and the Rise of Capitalism in the Connecticut Valley, 1800–1860." *Journal of Social History* 13, no. 2 (1979): 169–89.

——. *The Roots of Rural Capitalism: Western Massachusetts, 1780–1860.* Ithaca, N.Y.: Cornell University Press, 1990.

Cohen, Sheldon. "The Broken Bond: Divorce in Providence County, 1749–1809." *Rhode Island History* 44, no. 3 (1985): 67–79.

Cott, Nancy F. *The Bonds of Womanhood: "Woman's Sphere" in New England, 1780–1835.* New Haven, Conn.: Yale University Press, 1977.

——. "Divorce and the Changing Status of Women in Eighteenth-Century Massachusetts." *William and Mary Quarterly,* 3rd series 33, no. 4 (1976): 586–614.

——. "Eighteenth-Century Family and Social Life Revealed in Massachusetts

Divorce Records." In Nancy F. Cott and Elizabeth H. Pleck, eds., *A Heritage of Her Own: Towards a New Social History of American Women*. New York: Simon and Schuster, 1979. 107–35.

———. *Public Vows: A History of Marriage and the Nation*. Cambridge: Harvard University Press, 2000.

Curtin, Donna DeFabio. "'The *Gentlest*, the Most *Polished*, Most *Beautiful* Part of the Creation': Gender and Gentility in the Early Republic." Paper presented at the annual meeting of the Society for Historians of the Early American Republic, Cincinnati, Oh., July 22, 1995.

Daniels, Bruce C. *The Connecticut Town: Growth and Development, 1635–1790*. Middletown, Conn.: Wesleyan University Press, 1979.

Daniels, Christine, and Kennedy, Michael V., eds. *Over the Threshold: Intimate Violence in Early America*. New York: Routledge, 1999.

Davis, Lance E., et al. *American Economic Growth: An Economist's History of the United States*. New York: HarperCollins, 1972.

Dayton, Cornelia Hughes. *Women before the Bar: Gender, Law, and Society in Connecticut, 1639–1789*. Chapel Hill: University of North Carolina Press, 1995.

Degler, Carl N. *At Odds: Women and the Family in America from the Revolution to the Present*. New York: Oxford University Press, 1980.

De Wolfe, Elizabeth A. *Shaking the Faith: Women, Family, and Mary Marshall Dyer's Anti-Shaker Campaign, 1815–1867*. New York: Palgrave, 2002.

Faragher, John Mack. *Women and Men on the Overland Trail*. New Haven, Conn.: Yale University Press, 1979.

Ferris, Barbara B., and Grace Louise Knox, eds. *Connecticut Divorces: Superior Court Records for the Counties of Litchfield, 1752–1922, and Hartford, 1740–1849*. Bowie, Md.: Heritage Books, 1989.

Gilmore, William J. *Reading Becomes a Necessity of Life: Material and Cultural Life In Rural New England, 1780–1835*. Knoxville: University of Tennessee Press, 1989.

Goodheart, Lawrence B., Neil Hanks, and Elizabeth Johnson. "'An Act for the Relief of Females . . .': Divorce and the Changing Legal Status of Women in Tennessee, 1796–1860, Part 1." *Tennessee Historical Quarterly* 44, no. 3 (1985): 318–39.

———. "'An Act for the Relief of Females . . .': Divorce and the Changing Legal Status of Women in Tennessee, 1796–1860, Part 2." *Tennessee Historical Quarterly* 44, no. 4 (1985): 402–16.

Goodrich, John E. *The State of Vermont Rolls of the Soldiers in the Revolutionary War, 1775 to 1783*. Rutland, Vt.: Tuttle, 1904.

Goodwin, Joseph O. *East Hartford: Its History and Traditions*. Hartford, Conn., 1879; rpt. East Hartford, Conn.: Raymond Library Company, 1976.

Griswold, Robert L. "The Evolution of the Doctrine of Mental Cruelty in Victorian American Divorce, 1790–1800." *Journal of Social History* 20, no. 1 (1986): 127–48.

Gross, Robert A. "Culture and Cultivation: Agriculture and Society in Thoreau's Concord." *Journal of American History* 69, no. 1 (1982): 42–55.

Grossberg, Michael. *Governing the Hearth: Law and the Family in Nineteenth-Century America.* Chapel Hill: University of North Carolina Press, 1985.

Gundersen, Joan R. "Independence, Citizenship, and the American Revolution." *Signs* 13, no. 1 (1987): 59–77.

Gundersen, Joan R., and Gwen Victor Gampel. "Married Women's Legal Status in Eighteenth-Century New York and Virginia." *William and Mary Quarterly,* 3rd series, 39 (January 1982): 114–34.

Hall, David D. *Worlds of Wonder, Days of Judgment: Popular Religious Belief in Early New England.* Cambridge: Harvard University Press, 1989.

Hartog, Hendrik. *Man and Wife in America: A History.* Cambridge: Harvard University Press, 2000.

———. "Marital Exits and Marital Expectations in Nineteenth-Century America." *Georgetown Law Journal* 80, no. 1 (1991): 95–129.

Helmbrecht-Wilson, Stacy. "'Went a Shopping': Elite and Middling Women as Consumers in Massachusetts, 1790–1830." Ph.D. dissertation, Boston University, 1999.

Hemenway, Abby Maria, ed. *Vermont Historical Gazetteer.* 5 vols. Burlington, Vt., 1867–1891.

Herndon, Ruth Wallis. *Unwelcome Americans: Living on the Margin in Early New England.* Philadelphia: University of Pennsylvania Press, 2001.

Hoff, Joan. *Law, Gender, and Injustice: A Legal History of U.S. Women.* New York: New York University Press, 1991.

Isenberg, Nancy. *Sex and Citizenship in Antebellum America.* Chapel Hill: University of North Carolina Press, 1998.

Jabour, Anya. *Marriage in the Early Republic: Elizabeth and William Wirt and the Companionate Ideal.* Baltimore: Johns Hopkins University Press, 1998.

Jaffee, David. "One of the Primitive Sort: Portrait Makers in the Rural North, 1760–1860." In Steven Hahn and Jonathan Prude, eds., *The Countryside in the Age of Capitalist Transformation: Essays in the History of Rural America.* Chapel Hill: University of North Carolina Press, 1985. 103–38.

———. "Peddlers of Progress and the Transformation of the Rural North, 1760–1860." *Journal of American History* 78, no. 2 (1991): 511–35.

———. "The Village Enlightenment in New England, 1760–1820." *William and Mary Quarterly,* 3rd series, 47 (July 1990): 327–46.

Jensen, Joan M. *Loosening the Bonds: Mid-Atlantic Farm Women, 1750–1850.* New Haven, Conn.: Yale University Press, 1986.

Johnson, Paul E. "The Modernization of Mayo Greenleaf Patch: Land, Family, and Marginality in New England, 1766–1818." *New England Quarterly 55*, no. 4 (1982): 488–516.

Kelly, Catherine E. *In the New England Fashion: Reshaping Women's Lives in the Nineteenth Century.* Ithaca, N.Y.: Cornell University Press, 1999.

Keohler, Lyle. "The Case of the American Jezebels: Anne Hutchinson and Female Agitation during the Years of the Antinomian Turmoil, 1636–1640." *William and Mary Quarterly,* 3rd series, 31, no. 1 (1974): 55–78.

Kerber, Linda K. *No Constitutional Right to Be Ladies: Women and the Obligations of Citizenship.* New York: Hill and Wang, 1998.

————. "Separate Spheres, Female Worlds, Woman's Place: The Rhetoric of Women's History." *Journal of American History 75*, no. 1 (1988): 9–39.

————. *Women of the Republic: Intellect and Ideology in Revolutionary America.* Chapel Hill: University of North Carolina Press, 1980.

Kurth, Jan. "Wayward Wenches and Wives: Runaway Women in the Hudson Valley, N.Y., 1785–1830." *NWSA Journal 1* (Winter 1988–89): 199–220.

Lantz, Herman. "Marital Incompatibility and Social Change in Early America." *Sage Research Papers in the Social Sciences* no. 4, Series Number: 90-026. Studies of Marriage and the Family, 1976.

Lebsock, Suzanne. *The Free Women of Petersburg: Status and Culture in a Southern Town, 1784–1860.* New York: Norton, 1984.

Lewis, Jan. *The Pursuit of Happiness: Family and Values in Jefferson's Virginia.* Cambridge: Cambridge University Press, 1983.

————. "The Republican Wife: Virtue and Seduction in the Early Republic." *William and Mary Quarterly,* 3rd series, 44 (October 1987): 689–721.

Lockridge, Kenneth. *Literacy in Colonial New England.* New York: Norton, 1974.

Lovejoy, Evelyn M. Wood. *History of Royalton, Vermont, with Family Genealogies, 1769–1911.* Burlington, Vt.: Free Press Printing Co., 1911.

Lystra, Karen. *Searching the Heart: Women, Men, and Romantic Love in Nineteenth-Century America.* New York: Oxford University Press, 1989.

Matson, Cathy. "The Revolution, the Constitution, and the New Nation." In Stanley L. Engerman and Robert E. Gallum, eds., *The Cambridge Economic History of the United States.* 2 vols. New York: Cambridge University Press, 1996. 1:363–401.

Mintz, Steven, and Susan Kellog. *Domestic Revolutions: A Social History of American Family Life.* New York: Free Press, 1988.

Monaghan, E. Jennifer. "Literacy Instruction and Gender in Colonial New England." *American Quarterly 40,* no.1 (1988): 18–41.

Newton, William Monroe. *History of Barnard, Vermont with Family Genealogies, 1761–1927.* 2 Vols. Montpelier, Vt.: Vermont Historical Society, 1928.

Norton, Mary Beth. "'My Resting Reaping Times': Sarah Osborne's Defense of Her Unfeminine Activities." *Signs* 2, no. 2 (1976): 515–29.

Nylander, Jane C. "Provisions for Daughters: The Accounts of Samuel Lane." In Peter Benes, ed., *House and Home*. Annual Proceedings of the Dublin Seminar for New England Folklife, 1988. Boston: Boston University Press, 1990. 11–27.

Osterud, Nancy Grey. *Bonds of Community: The Lives of Farm Women in Nineteenth-Century New York*. Ithaca, N.Y.: Cornell University Press, 1991.

Phillips, Roderick. *Putting Asunder: A History of Divorce in Western Society*. Cambridge: Cambridge University Press, 1988.

Pleck, Elizabeth. *Domestic Tyranny: The Making of American Social Policy against Family Violence from Colonial Times to the Present*. New York: Oxford University Press, 1987.

Richardson, Frederick W. *Eighteenth-Century Springfield: From Wilderness to Vermont Statehood, 1751–1791*. Newport, N.H.: F. W. Richardson, 1991.

Riley, Glenda. *Divorce: An American Tradition*. New York: Oxford University Press, 1991.

Roth, Randolph A. *The Democratic Dilemma: Religion, Reform, and the Social Order in the Connecticut River Valley of Vermont, 1791–1850*. Cambridge: Cambridge University Press, 1987.

Rothman, Ellen K. *Hands and Hearts: A History of Courtship in America*. Cambridge: Harvard University Press, 1987.

Russell, Howard S. *A Long Deep Furrow: Three Centuries of Farming in New England*. Hanover, N.H.: University Press of New England, 1982.

Ryan, Mary P. *Cradle of the Middle Class: The Family in Oneida County, New York, 1790–1865*. Cambridge: Cambridge University Press, 1981.

Salmon, Marylynn. *Women and the Law of Property in Early America*. Chapel Hill: University of North Carolina Press, 1986.

Schultz, Martin. "Divorce in Early America: Origins and Patterns in Three North Central States." *Sociological Quarterly* 25, no. 4 (1984): 511–26.

Schwartzberg, Beverly. "'Lots of Them Did That': Desertion, Bigamy, and Marital Fluidity in Late-Nineteenth-Century America." *Journal of Social History* 37, no. 3 (2004): 573–600.

Shammas, Carole. *A History of Household Government in America*. Charlottesville: University of Virginia Press, 2002.

Sievens, Mary Beth. "Divorce, Patriarchal Authority, and Masculinity: A Case from Early National Vermont." *Journal of Social History* 37, no. 3 (2004): 651–61.

———. "'The Wicked Agency of Others': Community, Law, and Marital Conflict in Vermont, 1790–1830." *Journal of the Early Republic* 21, no. 1 (2001): 19–39.

Smith, Merril D. *Breaking the Bonds: Marital Discord in Pennsylvania, 1730–1830.* New York: New York University Press, 1991.

Smith-Rosenberg, Carroll. "The Female World of Love and Ritual: Relations between Women in Nineteenth-Century America." *Signs* 1, no. 1 (1975): 1–30.

Stansell, Christine. *City of Women: Sex and Class in New York, 1789–1860.* Chicago: University of Illinois Press, 1987.

Stein, Stephen J. *The Shaker Experience in America.* New Haven, Conn.: Yale University Press, 1992.

Stilwell, Lewis. *Migration from Vermont (1791–1860).* Montpelier: Vermont Historical Society, 1948.

Sword, Kirsten Denise. "Wayward Wives, Runaway Slaves, and the Limits of Patriarchal Authority in Early America." Ph.D. dissertation. Harvard University, 2002.

Taylor, Alan. "The Gendered Order of a Rural Village in the Early American Republic." Unpublished paper in the author's possession.

Thompson, Zadock. *A Gazetteer of the State of Vermont.* Montpelier, Vt., 1824.

Ulrich, Laurel Thatcher. "'A Friendly Neighbor': Social Dimensions of Daily Work in Northern New England." In Kathryn Kish Sklar and Thomas Dublin, eds., *Women and Power in American History: A Reader.* Vol. 1, *To 1800.* Englewood Cliffs, N.J.: Prentice Hall, 1991. 37–50.

———. *Good Wives: Image and Reality in the Lives of Women in Northern New England, 1650–1750.* New York: Vintage, 1980.

———. "Housewife and Gadder: Themes of Self-Sufficiency and Community in Eighteenth-Century New England." In Carol Groneman and Mary Beth Norton, eds., *"To Toil the Livelong Day": America's Women at Work, 1780–1980.* Ithaca, N.Y.: Cornell University Press, 1987. 21–34.

———. *A Midwife's Tale: The Life of Martha Ballard, Based on Her Diary, 1785–1812.* New York: Vintage, 1990.

———. "Wheels, Looms, and the Gender Division of Labor in Eighteenth-Century New England." *William and Mary Quarterly,* 3rd series, 55, no. 1 (1988): 3–38.

Waciega, Lisa Wilson. *Life after Death: Widows in Pennsylvania, 1750–1850.* Philadelphia: Temple University Press, 1992.

Ward, Barbara McLean. "Women's Property and Family Continuity in Eighteenth-Century Connecticut." In Peter Benes, ed., *Early American Probate Records.* The Dublin Seminar for New England Folklife Annual Proceedings, 1987. Boston: Boston University Press, 1989. 74–85.

Welter, Barbara. "The Cult of True Womanhood: 1820–1860." *American Quarterly,* 18 (1966): 151–74.

Index

About the Author

Mary Beth Sievens is Assistant Professor of History at SUNY Fredonia.